OBADIAH

A Critical Exegetical Commentary

OBADIAH

A Critical Exegetical Commentary

by

John D. W. Watts
Baptist Theological Seminary
Rüschlikon, Switzerland

ALPHA PUBLICATIONS
Winona Lake, Indiana 46590
1981

CONTENTS

PREFACE

This book began in the author's use of Obadiah to help students of Hebrew learn the purposes and forms of text criticism. Nearer acquaintance added appreciation. The application of basic form-historical methods to the study of the book and the problems of its interpretation brought some very satisfying results. Those studies became the backbone for a commentary.

Work on interpretation revealed a gap in material concerning the history of Edom, and an attempt has been made to fill that. The book of Obadiah has received far more than its share of hard judgment for its attitude toward the enemies of God's people. It is hoped that this commentary may put this in a proper light.

The author is grateful for the patience of several generations of students who studied earlier drafts of this material. Mr. Ray Hobbs, B.D., Th.M. from England, and Mr. Carlos Santin, B.D., Th.M. from Spain, have materially aided the work by preparing indices and reading proof.

May this little book help to throw light on the meaning of this shortest book of the Bible to the Glory of God.

JDWW

Rüschlikon, Switzerland

I

INTRODUCTION

A. REVIEW OF EARLIER WORKS

This smallest of the books in the Old Testament has earned disproportionate attention from the scholars.[1] George Adam Smith referred to it as an ideal place to test the methods of a sound criticism since it neither claims a date for itself nor deals with any important theological issue.[2] Perhaps this very fact has tempted students of holy writ to have their try at solving its problems.

The position of the book in the first part of the Twelve Prophets has been taken to indicate a date not later than the eighth century.[3] The name of the prophet, if it is a name, has been used to relate the book to known bearers of the name.[4] Yet the deep problems which the book raises for the student have turned on other issues.

The book purports to be a prophecy against Edom and for a reconstitution of Israel on her own soil. It alludes ambiguously to historical events that are evidently past (vv. 10ff. and 16) and predicts events that presuppose certain fixed situations in the history

1. The latest critical commentary in English is by J. A. Bewer, *ICC* (1911). Pertinent earlier literature is listed there, pp. 17–18. In German the critical commentaries of Sellin, *KAT*[3] (1929), and T. H. Robinson, *HAT* (1939[2], 1954). Smaller and more popular treatments are by Weiser, *ATD* (1949[2], 1956); Thompson, *IB* (1956); Brockington, *Peake's Commentary on the Bible* (1962); Ziegler, *Old Testament Commentary* (1948); D. W. B. Robinson, *New Bible Commentary* (1953); Livingston, *Wycliffe Bible Commentary* (1962); Eaton, *Torch* (1961); Myers, *Layman's* (1959). Newer introductions referred to include those of Archer, B. Anderson, G. W. Anderson, Bentzen, Eissfeldt, Kuhl, Pfeiffer, Rowley, Weiser, Unger, and Young.
2. *The Book of the Twelve Prophets, EB*, p. 163.
3. C. F. Keil, 'The Twelve Minor Prophets,' *Biblical Commentary on the Old Testament*, I, 339.
4. The servant of Ahab, I Kings 18 : 1–16; a teacher of the law under Jehoshaphat, II Chron. 17 : 7 (Delitzsch); an overseer under Josiah, II Chron. 34 : 12; and others.

of both Edom and Judah (vv. 5–8 and 19–20). Criticism has usually hinged on attempts to solve the riddle of historical allusions in the book.

The event referred to in verses 10ff. and 16 in which Edom participated, or at least during which she stood idly by, a sacking of Jerusalem, has been identified with three separate periods. The earliest is that of Jehoshaphat (872–852 BC).[5] II Chronicles 20 records a battle with Moab, Ammon, and Edom in which Judah reaped the rewards of an unearned victory.[6] However, there is no word about a sack of Jerusalem or anything faintly resembling the description in Obadiah. The account is omitted in Kings, but may validly record the kind of unrest among these vassal peoples which would bear fruit in successful revolt against his son Jehoram (852–845 BC).[7] II Kings 8:20–22/II Chronicles 21:8–10 records the successful revolt of Edom from the rule of Judah, which continued, as the writers noted laconically, 'to this day.'[8] But no details are furnished that might explain the tirade in Obadiah. Yet these events have provided and do provide the historical background for Obadiah in the eyes of many interpreters.

The third suggestion is that of the destruction of Jerusalem in 586 BC.[9] This time the city was plundered and refugees were cut off in flight (II Kings 25:3–7). A month passed between the fall and the burning of the city[10] – a month probably devoted to plunder by the conquerors. Some biblical references apparently point to Edom's entering the battle on the side of Babylon.[11]

There can be little doubt that the catastrophe of 586 provides

---

5. Caspari, Ewa l, Graf, Pusey, Driver, Giesebrecht, Wildboer, and König.
6. T. H. Robinson, *A History of Israel*, I, 297.
7. Delitzsch, Keil, Volz, Orelli, Kirkpatrick, von Hofmann, Peters, (probably also Young), Unger.
8. J. Bright, *A History of Israel*, p. 229.
9. G. A. Smith, Hitzig, Kent, Rowley, G. W. Anderson, B. Anderson, Robinson, Rudolph, Weiser, Eissfeldt, Pfeiffer, Kuhl, Bentzen, Thompson.
10. R. Kittel, *Geschichte des Volkes Israel*, II, 546; M. Noth, *The History of Israel*, Eng. tr., p. 286.
11. Lam. 4 : 21f. Cp. Ps. 137 : 7 with Obad. 10–14; Bright, *op. cit.*, p. 308.

a better explanation for this section of Obadiah than the others –
a fact recognized by most modern interpreters and some not so
modern.[12]

Verses 19–20 are obviously predictions. Yet they equally obviously presuppose a situation in which great portions of the land
are in foreign hands as well as great portions of the population in
exile. They also seem to presuppose a time when Edom contemp-
tuously looks down on a prostrate Judah. Exegetes seem unable
to find a date short of the Exile that fits these qualifications, and
most of them would set dates in the early fourth century.[13] The
problem is particularly complicated by the appearance of the place
name Sepharad for the home of Judaean exiles. It has been vari-
ously located in Spain,[14] in southwest Media,[15] in Asia Minor,[16]
and more recently in Libya.[17] It is otherwise unknown to us in
biblical sources.

The historical situation that verses 5–8 reflect has also caused
considerable speculation. Wellhausen took them as referring to
things that had already happened and identified the events in terms
of incursions of Arab tribes in the fifth century.[18] This led him to
date the whole book in that time. However, most interpreters have
properly recognized the predictive character of these verses. One
impatiently shrugs off the issue with the words: 'We know in this
time (shortly after 586) no concrete occasion, but we need none.
The occasion is simply the faith in a just God who will avenge his
people.'[19]

Such varying dates for different parts of the book inevitably
pose the question of unity. A number of scholars have held un-

12. Calvin (quoted by G. A. Smith) thought it impossible for the book
to be earlier than Isaiah. See his comments on vv. 18–20.
13. Sellin, Pfeiffer, etc. But see Thompson, *IB*, V, 859.
14. Syr, Targ Jonathan, Ibn Ezra, Qimchi.
15. Schrader, Friedrich Delitzsch, Lenormant, G. A. Smith.
16. Mentioned in Persian inscriptions: de Sacy, Gesenius, Hitzig, Kuenen, W. R. Smith, Sayce, Barton, Sellin, Thompson.
17. John Gray, 'The Diaspora of Israel and Judah in Obadiah v. 20,'
ZAW, 65 (1953), 57ff.
18. Wellhausen.
19. W. Rudolph, 'Obadja,' *ZAW*, 49 (1931), 229.

waveringly to its unity,[20] but beginning with Eichhorn a growing number have sought to solve its vexing problems of interpretation by postulating a number of independent units of varying dates which have here been brought together.[21] Others would simply separate verses 19–21 as a later addition to the book.[22] Still others think of an original portion including verses 1–14 and 15b, with later additions in verses 15a, 16–18 and 19–21.[23] Robinson considers the book a collection of no less than seven separate oracles on a common theme (vv. 1–5, 6–7, 8–11, 12–14, 15–16, 17–18, 19–21).

Other questions concerning its literary integrity are posed by the parallel to verses 1b–5 in Jeremiah 49:14–16 and 9.[24] The question as to which has prior claim to originality or whether both are dependent on a third source has at least kept the problem of unity very much alive. A number of affinities to the book of Joel[25] have usually been explained as dependence of Joel on Obadiah. But these also have served to emphasize the possibility of composite form.

These and other considerations have served to bring the little book into disrepute. It has been branded a sordid example of petty Jewish nationalism and hatred.[26] It has been castigated for its lack of charity and compared to disadvantage with the *'ebed Jahweh* of Isaiah 53.[27]

---

20. Delitzsch, Keil, Volz, Orelli, Kirkpatrick, Pusey, König, von Hofmann, Peters, Unger, Young, and others.
21. Wellhausen, Nowack, Cornill, Duhm, Gray, Marti, Haupt, Ewald, Kuenen, Wildboer, Driver, Smith, Kautzsch, Bewer, Barton, etc.
22. Rudolph, Weiser, Orelli.
23. Eissfeldt, Pfeiffer.
24. H. Bekel,' Ein vorexilisches Orakel über Edom in der Klagestrophe – die gemeinsame Quelle von Obadja 1–9 und Jeremiah 49 : 7–22,' *Theologische Studien und Kritiken*, 80 (1907), 315–343.
25. Obad.   1 – Joel 3 : 9 (4 : 9)
    „   10 – „   3 : 19 (4 : 19)
    „   11 – „   3 : 3 (4 : 3)
    „   15 – „   1 : 15, 3 (4) : 4, 7, 14
    „   17 – „   (3 : 5), 3 : 17 (4 : 17).
26. G. A. Smith, *The Book of the Twelve Prophets*, p. 172, and others.
27. R. H. Pfeiffer, *Introduction to the Old Testament* (1941), p. 586.

Recently the growing influence of form criticism (or better, *Traditions Historie*) has made itself felt in the study of Obadiah.[28] The historical relationships and allusions are played down or discounted altogether. 'Edom' is understood as a pseudonym for the powers of chaos, and the whole is placed within the frame of the cosmic struggle pictured in the New Year's festival. The supposed *Sitz im Leben* is the familiar pattern propagated by the Uppsala school. The method offers a number of attractive possibilities, not the least of which are the possibilities to show a unity of material and purpose (even if the origin of particular parts is diverse) and an emphasis of ideas and ideology which would justify the book's having been included in the Canon. But it suffers through exaggeration of extravagant imagery and is vitiated by a view of Israel's cult that is plainly untenable. An adequate treatment of the prophecy of Obadiah must fulfill three requirements:[29] (1) it must deal seriously with historical allusions in the book; (2) it must determine the place and classification of Obadiah within biblical prophecy; and (3) it must ascertain the position the book occupied in Israelitic worship.

B. A HISTORY OF EDOM

A satisfactory history of Edom and the Edomites does not exist. The references in the ancient sources are meager and scattered,[30] and those in modern works are not much better.[31] The subject has awakened the interest of a number of people, however, and

28. M. Bič, 'Ein verkanntes Thronbesteigungsfestorakel im A. T.,' *Auchin Orientalni*, xix (1962), Prague, pp. 568–578. M. Bič, 'Zur Problematik des Obadjah,' *SVT*, I (1963), 11–25. I. Engnell, 'Obadjas bok,' *Svenskt Bibliskt Uppslagsverk*, II (1962²), cols. 358–361.
29. In addition, of course, to the normal care of textual criticism, adequate translation, etc.
30. II Maccabees 5 : 8; Diodorus, *Bibliotheka*, XIX, 94; Records of Marneptah and Rameses III (Breasted, *Ancient Records of Egypt*, III, 273 and IV, 201), as well as the biblical references. See Noth, *op. cit.*, p. iii, n. 4.
31. The only book on the subject, Buhl, *Die Geschichte der Edomiter* (1893), is completely out of date. Dictionary and encyclopedia articles are hardly adequate for this purpose.

their work is recorded in articles and monographs.[32]

Edom is the name of a territory adjacent to Judah which bore at various times for biblical writers the names Seir,[33] Hor (Num. 20–21 and Deut. 32:50), Edom,[34] or Esau (Jer. 49, Deut. 2, and Obad. Gen. 36:8[?]). In pre-exilic times it appears to have had the *'Arabah* as its western border,[35] although the references are not always consistent. Some scholars have maintained that Edom claimed land still further to the west.[36] The *'Arabah* is no real natural boundary, but rather forms a passage,[37] which may account for the discrepancy in accounts.

The brook Zered (Isa. 15:7; Deut. 2:13) formed the northern boundary. This was a very real and natural division since it separated two very different kinds of territory. To the north stretched the plateau of Moab. To the south rose the highlands of Edom.[38] These highlands are characterized by red sandstone cliffs that rise east of the Dead Sea and *'Arabah* in three great steps to the impressive height of more than 5,000 feet above sea level. This rugged territory is very inaccessible and easily fortified. The southern frontier is marked by the Negeb, which runs southeast from *'Ain Sharandel* in the *'Arabah*.[39] The desert marks the eastern boundary. The whole, east of the *'Arabah,* is not more than 112 by 20 to 30 miles.[40]

32. Such as: F.-M. Abel, 'L'expédition dés Grecs à Pétra en 312 avant J.-C.,' *RB*, 46 (1937), 372–391; H. Grimme, 'Der Untergang Edoms,' *Die Welt als Geschichte*, 3 (1937), 452–463; Starcky, 'The Nabateans,' *BA*, XVIII (1955), 84–106; V. Maag, 'Jakob-Esau-Edom,' *TZ*, 13 (1957), 418–429; N. Glueck, 'The Boundaries of Edom,' *HUCA*, XI (1936), 141–157.
33. 34 times from Gen. 14 through Ezek. 35.
34. 83 times throughout the Old Testament but not in Lev. nor Deut.
35. Cf. Glueck, *op. cit.*, p. 157; J. Simons, *The Geographical and Topographical Texts of the Old Testament* (1959), p. 24. On the relation of this name to the others see Maag, *op. cit.*
36. Buhl, *op. cit.*, pp. 22, 24, 26; G. B. Gray, *Numbers*, *ICC*, p. 266; Driver, *Deuteronomy*, p. 30; G. A. Smith, *The Historical Geography of the Holy Land* (25th ed., 1931), p. 560; Abel, *Géographie de la Palestine*, I (1933), 281–284, 389–391; and others.
37. Smith, *op. cit.*
38. D. Baly, *The Geography of the Bible* (1957), pp. 240–241.
39. *Ibid.*, p. 242.
40. Smith, *op. cit.*, p. 562.

In the north and east there are areas for fruitful cultivation. But the land derived its significance and its wealth from its strategic position astride the trade routes between Syria and Egypt. G. A. Smith called it a land of passage.[41] Its inhabitants grew rich and strong on the tolls exacted from transient merchant caravans (Isa. 21:13, 14; Job 6:19; Ezek. 27:15, 21–22; Amos 1:6–9; Gen. 37:25). Edom's major cities included Teman in the south and Bozrah in the north. Sela[42] was a small but famous forerunner of the well-known and oft-visited fortifications of Petra[43] of later fame.

The earliest inhabitants of this territory known to biblical writers were Horites.[44] This non-Semitic people has in recent times become familiar to archaeologists as Hurrians.[45] The excavations at Nuzi and Boghaz-koy have enabled scholars to piece together their history.[46]

Earliest traces of the people can be found in the third milennium BC. They had their home in the neighborhood of Lake Van in northern Syria. From there they expanded southward in the second millennium and founded the Hurrian kingdom of Mittani in northern Mesopotamia. The history of Mittani can now be sketched from its obscure beginnings about 1500 BC to its absorption by the Assyrian empire some two hundred years later.[47]

During this period of power, Hurrian expansion reached as far south as Egypt. The Horites to whom the Bible refers were evi-

41. *Ibid.*, p. 561.
42. Baly, *op. cit.*, p. 245.
43. Cf. S. Cohen, 'Petra,' *IDB*, III, 772–3.
44. Gen. 36 (and 14); Deut. 2 : 12, 22. But Albright and Glueck have argued that Horites (Hurrians) did not inhabit Edom. Cf. W. F. Albright, 'The Horites in Palestine,' in Leary (ed.), *From the Pyramids to Paul* (New York: Nelson, 1935), p. 22; N. Glueck, *op. cit.*, 141. Glueck's findings make it probable that Hurrian occupation occurred between 2000 and 1800 BC or not at all. This period would neatly fit the dates of Hurrian expansion suggested by I. J. Gelb, *Hurrians and Subarians* (Chicago, 1944), p. 89.
45. Gelb, *op. cit.;* E. A. Speiser, 'Introduction to Hurrian,' *AASOR* (1941); *Journal of World History*, I (1953), 311–327.
46. Cf. E. A. Speiser, 'Hurrians,' *IDB*, II, 664–5.
47. N. Glueck, *op. cit.*

dently a pocket of such Hurrian advance. As Hurrian power retrogressed, its peoples were absorbed into local cultures and populations. Thus for centuries afterwards scattered Hurrian names appear in many diverse places in the Near East including Palestine. However, in the territory east of Jordan they have left no traces permanent enough for the archaeologists' picks to recover. Apparently they were succeeded in this area by nomads who dominated it until the thirteenth century BC. This period of nomadic dominance, suggested by archaeological survey, roughly fits the biblical references to Esau and his tribes both as to character and as to date (Gen. 36). The development of a settled culture with cities first came in the thirteenth century through a people known specifically as Edomites.[48]

The Edomites had firm possession of the land by the time of Israel's exodus from Egypt (Num. 20:14–21; 21:4). They were clearly a Semitic people who were in some way related to Israel (or at least to the southern tribes of Israel).[49] They, like Israel's fathers, had probably migrated from the northeast. The biblical evidence would point to a strong tribal organization during Jacob's time (Gen. 36:15–30), which had become a kingdom long before a similar change took place in Israel.[50]

Apparently Edom was famous in early times for its wisdom.[51] Job's comforters were from Edom,[52] and it is likely that some names mentioned in Proverbs refer to Edomite princes.[53]

Despite the difficulties that the Edomites placed in the path of the migrating Israelites during their wilderness journeys (Num. 20:14–21), the Israelites appear to have lived as peaceful neighbors to them until the reign of Saul. They may have had points of contact such as the common use of sanctuaries like that at Beer-

---

48. *Ibid.*; *BASOR*, 55 (1934), 3–21; and *AASOR*, XV (1951), 137–140.
49. The Kenites appear both in Israel and in Edom (Gen. 36 : 11, 15, 42; Josh. 14 : 6, 14; 15 : 17); Glueck, *HUCA*, XI, 147f. The clan of Serach belongs to Simeon according to Num. 26 : 13, but to Edom in Gen. 36 : 13, 33. This is also surely the meaning in the Jacob–Esau stories as well, esp. Gen. 25.
50. Gen. 36 : 31–39. M. Noth, *The History of Israel* (1958), p. 154.
51. 'Cut off the wise man from Edom' Obad. 8.
52. Job 4 : 1 — 'the Temanite.'
53. Prov. 30 : 1 and 31 : 1 – 'Massa.'

sheba.[54] In these matters clans who claimed kinship to both groups, like the Kenites, must have played particularly important roles. The Kenites occupied that strategic border land which was so rich in minerals that it became a major source of rivalry between the two peoples.[55]

Friendly co-existence came to a brutal end in David's subjection of the Edomites in the valley of salt. The brief account in II Samuel recounts 18,000 dead and garrisons established throughout the country (II Sam. 8:13–14). Kings tells of a six-month campaign carried out by Joab to destroy every male, especially all of the royal house.[56] David then apparently enslaved the Edomites to work the copper mines of the region.[57]

Until this time Edom must have been thought of as Israel's 'elder brother' in being stronger, older, and more developed. By this battle 'the elder' was 'supplanted' by 'the younger' in clear historical analogy to the Jacob–Esau parallel in Genesis.[58] From this point on one can trace the bitter rivalry which is documented in the prophecy of Obadiah.

The victory of David over Edom was important in many ways. It not only gave him access to the important copper mines of the *'Arabah,* but also assured access to the Gulf of 'Akabah and the Red Sea as well as protection to the southeast flank of David's empire.[59] Solomon attempted to continue his father's policy regarding Edom, but with only partial success. One prince had escaped Joab's blood bath. He now returned and gained possession of a part of the old kingdom of Edom.[60] This fits the picture of Solomon's gradual loss of the power he had inherited. Despite the division of the kingdom on the accession of Rehoboam and the

54. A. Alt, *Der Gott der Väter* (1929), reprinted in *Kleine Schriften,* I (1953), 60; K. Galling, 'Gemeindegesetz in Deut. 23,' *Bertholet Festschrift* (1950), p. 181.
55. Glueck, *op. cit.,* pp. 147f.
56. I Kings 11 : 15, 17. One royal son, Hadad, apparently escaped to Egypt. Cf. E. Meyer, *Die Israeliten und ihre Nachbarstämmen* (1906), pp. 355ff.; Galling, *op. cit.,* p. 182.
57. Glueck, *op. cit.,* p. 148.
58. Maag, *op. cit.,* pp. 425–426.
59. M. Noth, *op. cit.,* p. 195.
60. I Kings 11 : 14–22, 25a. Noth, *op. cit.,* pp. 204–5.

re-establishment of a dissident group in Edom, she remained to some extent under Judah.[61]

Solomon almost certainly ran the copper mines with Edomite and Canaanite slave labor.[62] The Edomites at a later period also had a reputation for slave-running (Amos 1:6, 9), and on occasion took slaves from Judah (II Chron. 28:17). The end of Solomon's era[63] seems to have brought a cessation of trading activity. Edom does not appear in the history again until the days of Jehoshaphat (872–852 BC), when it was being ruled by a deputy governor.[64] Apparently Judah had maintained sovereignty over Edom and had worked the copper mines. This dependency is well illustrated by the story in II Kings 3 where Joram and Jehoshaphat have the help of the 'king' of Edom in a war against Moab.

However, this dependency upon Judah was soon to come to an end. A raid on Judah by certain Edomite forces against Engedi during the reign of Jehoshaphat illustrates the beginning of trouble (II Chron. 20). Joram, Jehoshaphat's son, bore the brunt of the Edomite rebellion. During his reign they put a king in the place of the former deputy governor and re-established their independence (II Kings 8:20–22).

This period of independence lasted some fifty years until Amaziah of Judah defeated it, capturing Sela and renaming it Joktheel (II Kings 14:7; II Chron. 25:11–12). Uzziah continued his father's work by recovering Elath from Edom and making it into a port (II Chron. 26:1–2; II Kings 14:22). Judah's domination continued in the reign of Ahaz. Edom then took advantage of Judah's involvement in the Syro-Ephraimitic war to regain her independence.[65] Judah was never again strong enough to take the 'Arabah and its riches.

61. Ibid., p. 226.
62. Cf. his methods in other areas: I Kings 5 : 27–30; 9 : 20–21.
63. The best account of Edomite—Judaean history for the period of the Divided Kingdom known to this writer is that by Glueck, op. cit., pp. 149–152. The present account follows his very closely.
64. I Kings 22 : 48. For a note on the discrepancy with II Kings 3 : 9, 12, cf. Glueck, op. cit., p. 149, n. 42.
65. Glueck, probably correctly, accepts Eissfeldt's emendation of II Kings 16 : 6, reading Edom for Aram (Die Heilige Schrift des A.T., 4th ed., ad loc.).

During Assyrian ascendency Edom was a vassal like all her neighbors. Kaush-malak was a vassal to Tiglath-Pileser III (744–727), Malik-ram to Sennacherib (705–681), Kaush-gabr to Psarhaddon (681–668) and Asshurbanipal (668–626).[66]

Near the beginning of the sixth century, as Jerusalem falls before the Babylonian invader, Edom along with Ammon and Moab are independent states.[67] Edom evidently escaped the fate of Judah since Jeremiah 40:11 tells of many Judaeans fleeing there in 587 BC. But the end was not far off. Josephus[68] says that Nebuchadnezzar subjugated the Ammonites and the Moabites five years after the capture of Jerusalem and in the twenty-third year of his reign.[69] Whether Edom also met her fate at this time, we can only conjecture. Her final end 'remains shrouded in mystery.'[70]

The province of Edom had already been ceded a portion of southern Judah as early as 598 BC, and in the period of Nehemiah (Neh. 3) Edom was understood to be on both sides of the *Arabah* as indeed it generally is pictured in postexilic writings.[71]

Writings of this postexilic period picture Edom's conduct on the occasion of the fall of Jerusalem (597 BC) in blackest terms. She is pictured as rejoicing in the fall and sharing in the plunder and perhaps even in the slaughter of her people (Isa. 63:1–6; Joel 3:19; Mal. 1:4. Cf. also Ecclus. 50:26).

At some time in the fifth century Edom passed from the scene as a nation.[72] Nehemiah was opposed by his neighbors, but in the place where one would expect Edom to be named only Geshem, the Arab, is named (Neh. 6:1). This had led to the assumption that the Edomites were overcome by Arabian tribes.[73]

A more specific identification has been made by Hubert

66. Wade, *WC* on Obad., p. xix.
67. Noth, *op. cit.*, p. 292. Jer. 27 : 3 implies that kings still reigned there in the fourth year of Zedekiah.
68. *Antiq. of the Jews*, X, 9, 7, pp. 181f. in Niese.
69. Noth, *op. cit.*, sees this confirmed in the inscriptions of Nebuchadnezzar from the Wadi Brisa.
70. *Ibid.*, p. 293.
71. Noth, *op. cit.*, p. 325; Glueck, *op. cit.*, pp. 154f.
72. Nelson Glueck has shown Edom to have been without sedentary occupation in the Persian period: *AASOR*, XV (1935), 138ff.
73. Wellhausen and others.

Grimme (Mal. 1). He would place the conquest as some decades before 450 BC.[74] It did not come about from the Nabataeans, but by Lihjans,[75] a northwest Arabian people coming from a place of the same name near Dedan. He would even identify Geshem, the Arab, with the Lihjan name Gashm, which belonged to a Lihjan king, as well as a mayor.

By the year 312 BC the area was controlled by the Nabataeans.[76] In that year the Macedonians attempted to dislodge them, but failed. Excellent up-to-date studies of the Nabataeans and their history are given by Abel[77] and Starcky.[78] The tribe was apparently of pure nomadic character, but it gave up its original culture to assume the Aramaic language and culture of the sedentary population. The history of the area, then called Idumaea, was closely linked to that of Palestine at the beginning of the Christian era, and finally ceased to have an autonomous existence at the beginning of the second millennium AD.

Three questions of historical importance for the date and interpretation of Obadiah must be raised against the background of this historical sketch.

First, when did strong feeling against Edom develop in Israel? One must be aware that it was not always so, for there are many evidences of a brotherly feeling toward this people (Job; Gen. 33; Deut. 23:7–8). Max Haller judged its beginning to be found in the tragic events of 586 BC,[79] to which several biblical references refer. Viktor Maag thinks it began much earlier, and that it can be dated from David's conquest on.[80] Some would take the Jacob–Esau rivalry to witness to a still earlier and ingrained antipathy.

74. 'Der Untergang Edoms,' *Die Welt als Geschichte*, 3 (1957), 452–463. Cf. also J. Starcky, 'The Nabataeans: A Historical Sketch,' *BA*, XVIII (1955), 86; and W. F. Albright, 'Dedan,' *Geschichte und Altes Testament* (*Alt Festschrift*) (1953), pp. 1–12.
75. Starcky suggests the tribe of Qedan (biblical Kedar), p. 86.
76. Diodorus, *Bibliotheka*, II, 48 and XIX, 94–100.
77. F.-M. Abel, 'L'expédition dés Grecs à Pétra en 312 avant J.-C.,' *RB*, 46 (1937), 373ff.
78. 'The Nabataeans: A Historical Sketch,' *BA*, XVIII (1955), 84–106.
79. 'Edom im Urteil der Propheten,' *Marti Festschrift*, *BZAW*, 41 (1925), 102–117.
80. *Op. cit.*

Galling has suggested that the feeling may have been much more negative in the south even in earlier times due to difficulties about a common border while the warmer feelings of brotherhood lived on in the Jacob tribes of the north.[81]

The possibilities for bad feelings, especially with Judah, existed throughout the period of the kingdom. It seems clear, however, that this was intensified after 587 BC. This must also be about the time when Edom took on eschatological significance for the prophets.[82]

The second question is, When did Edom actually fall? As noted above, this is shrouded in mystery.[83] In 586 BC she was apparently still an independent state. By the time of Nehemiah (*ca.* 450 BC) she apparently no longer existed. Malachi's prophecy (Mal. 1:2) also seems to indicate that the destruction had already taken place. The likelihood is that Edom's fall came early in the fifth century, or even as early as the latter part of the sixth.[84]

The third question concerns the period when conditions mentioned in Obadiah 20 would have been possible. They apparently presuppose groups from the dispersion returning to reoccupy portions of the land. This obviously assumes that the Exile is already a reality. But our knowledge of conditions in various parts of the dispersion is too fragmentary to pin down a more definite date.[85]

A date for Obadiah in the early postexilic period – the end of the sixth or the first half of the fifth century BC – would fit the requirements of all three.

C. OBADIAH'S POSITION IN BIBLICAL PROPHECY

Most recent interpretation has tended to despise Obadiah as an expression of hateful and narrow nationalism.[86] In view of this interpretation it is a temptation to ask how the little book found

81. *Op. cit.*
82. See below, pp. 22–23.
83. See above, p. 17.
84. Note again Glueck's observation that Edom was not occupied by a sedentary people during the Persian period.
85. See discussion above on pp. 17–18 and the commentary on the passage.
86. Cf. Brockington and others.

its way into the Canon at all. Its position in Old Testament prophecy reflects nothing of this low esteem.

The compilers of prophetic traditions surely had abundant materials to choose from. Each of the works selected to be recorded and transmitted to posterity was chosen for good reasons. Obadiah has maintained its integrity as a separate prophecy, rather than simply being tacked onto another group. It has been accorded a position in the first half of the Book of the Twelve along with such giants as Hosea, Amos, and Micah for reasons best known to the compiler. But its having been preserved and granted this place among the great and timeless records of 'God's servants' indicates an acceptance and evaluation reaching far beyond the judgment of a compiler or editor.

The interpreter today must evaluate this acceptance of Obadiah first in the light of the standards that the compilers of the prophetic books applied which led them to judge this an authentic piece of Israelitic, or better, Jahwistic, prophecy.

What kind of prophecy is this? Interpretation has at times stressed its unity,[87] but it has often been felt necessary to show the divisions and differences in the book.[88] It is obviously a collection of oracles as most prophetic books are. These have been arranged in the form of a prophetic liturgy. They include a vision (v. 1); two oracles announcing the judgment to come (one in *qinah* 3–2 meter, vv. 1d–4, and one in regular 3–3 meter, vv. 5–10); an oracular deprecation (vv. 11–14); a 'Day of Jahweh' oracle (vv. 15–16); and a closing oracle in the form 'in those days' (vv. 17–21).

The order and form of this arrangement of oracles is similar to that in other prophetic passages.[89] The book should, therefore, be studied as a liturgical unity. But this does not necessarily mean that all of it was originally composed at the same time. The parallelism between certain verses and Jeremiah and parallel phrases to other prophecies indicates that they both could draw on a common fund of prophetic tradition in constructing a particular passage. But

87. Cf. above, p. 9, n. 20.
88. Cf. above, p. 10, n. 21 and p. 10, n. 23.
89. Like Amos, chap. 8. Cf. the author's *Vision and Prophecy in Amos* (1958), p. 45.

the whole is meaningful only as all of it is studied in the interrelation of its parts and in its proper *Sitz im Leben.*

If one uses the outline drawn from the analysis of passages in Amos,[90] the outline of Obadiah is as follows:

I. The Vision (v. 1b): A messenger is sent to summon the nations against Edom.
II. The Key Word or Motto (vv. 2–4): Proud Edom will be humbled. Verses 5–10 expand and intensify the theme: Edom will be completely destroyed.
III. Indictment and Deprecation (vv. 11–14): Edom's actions on Israel's day of troubles have sealed her fate.
IV. God's judgment day is near when Edom will be judged (vv. 15–16, and perhaps v. 18).
V. 'In those days' (vv. 17–21): the resulting situation.

Note that theological explanations are scattered in oracles II (vv. 5–9), III (v. 16), and V (v. 21).

The book turns on two phrases: 'to Edom' and 'the Day of Jahweh.' The first identifies the work as a 'foreign prophecy,' while the second provides the clue to its *Sitz im Leben.*

Foreign prophecies are a familiar form in the prophetic books of the Old Testament. Each of the three great books of prophecy contains a group of foreign prophecies (Isa. 13–23; Jer. 46–51; Ezek. 25–32). Amos begins with a collection of such prophecies in one speech (Amos 1–2). Nahum is such a prophecy against Assyria.

Among foreign prophecies, those against Edom are prominent. Each of the major collections contains one (Isa. 21:11–12; Jer. 49:7–22; Ezek. 25:12–14; Amos 1:11–12). In addition, she is mentioned a number of times in other passages (Joel 4:19; Mal. 1:2–5; Zech. 9:5ff.; Isa. 14:30f. (if Philistia is read as Edom); Isa. 34; Ezek. 32:29; 35; Isa. 63:1–6; Ps. 60:8, 9; 137:7; I Sam. 4:22). Edom seems to be one of the peoples that was regularly or always mentioned in foreign prophecies. It is also worth noting that Edom assumes eschatological significance as the symbol of total opposition to the Kingdom of God in some passages (Isa. 63:1–6; Joel

90. *Ibid.*

21

3:19 [Hebrew chap. 4:19]). This occurs so often that one scholar speaks of 'stereotyped curses against Edom after 587 BC.'[91]

It cannot be doubted that there is a clear development in the manner in which Edom is dealt with in these oracles. In the earlier form, as in Amos 1:11–12, Edom is simply one among several nations, neither better nor worse than the others. In later forms this is no longer the case, until finally Edom stands alone as the great symbol of 'anti-Jahweh' (Isa. 63:1–6).

Obadiah apparently belongs neither to the beginnings of this development nor to the most acute stage of eschatological denunciation. Here Edom is no longer one among many. She stands alone as the recipient of God's wrath and judgment. The intensity of feeling is much stronger, and she is specifically charged with crimes against Israel. Yet one hardly feels the eschatological dimension of Isaiah 63:1–6.

It has sometimes been suggested that foreign prophecies are prophecies of salvation in contrast to those which announce judgment for Israel.[92] But such a distinction is too simple. That such judgment does achieve for Israel a salvation from oppression is undeniable. But the very usage of the book of Amos, where such foreign prophecies lead up to a violent denunciation of Israel itself, should be a warning against dividing the two too sharply.

The second distinguishing phrase identifies the ritual and theological frame for the prophecy. It concerns the 'Day of Jahweh,' This theme is the foundation of all prophetic eschatology.[93] It was also the theme of the festival of covenant judgment and renewal which is currently often called the 'New Year's festival.'[94] Through long stretches of Israel's history this was the major festival of the year and incorporated a number of diverse elements. During the kingdom it provided expression for royal ideology, including themes of the Kingdom of God and creation. It also pro-

---

91. A. Bentzen, *Introduction*, II, 143.
92. A. Weiser, *The Old Testament: Its Formation and Development* (1961), p. 249.
93. L. Černy, 'The Day of Jahweh and Some Relevant Problems,' *Prace Z Vedeckych Ustavu* (Prague, 1948); H. W. Robinson, 'The Day of Jahweh,' *Inspiration and Revelation in the Old Testament* (Oxford, 1946).
94. Cf. Mowinckel, *Psalmenstudien*, II (Christiania, 1921–24).

vided the roots for Israelitic eschatology.[95] It was the place and time at which many prophetic oracles were enunciated.

This suggests that the prophecy of Obadiah was presented during such a festival in the dramatic celebration of covenant judgment. The relation of the various themes within the books can best be explained by this setting. They suggest a theological basis much more profound than the national prejudice and hatred that has so often been attributed to it.

The themes of 'the Kingdom of Jahweh' and 'the Day of Jahweh' are basic to Israel's New Year's festival as they are to the book of Obadiah and to Old Testament theology as a whole. The judgment that was pronounced was based on an understanding of the reign of Jahweh which expressed itself in a special way on his day. The punishment of Edom and the restoration of Israel were means by which that reign was to be realized in history.

What kind of prophet prepared or spoke these words? Current scholarship has recognized the complexity of the problem, for there were various kinds of prophets as there were various kinds of prophecy. We have learned to speak of cult prophets as those who performed prophetic functions within established ritual. If the occasion for such prophetic liturgy as Obadiah was that of festal ritual, then the author of these oracles should properly be called a 'cult prophet.' Yet this should in nowise detract from our estimation of his inspiration or his authority as a man of God.[96]

Such a prophet undoubtedly drew on older prophetic tradition in composing his material. Apparently both this anonymous prophet and Jeremiah drew on the same traditional material.[97]

All these factors support Obadiah's claim to a place among the canonical prophets: its accepted liturgical form, its character as a foreign prophecy, its nature as a judgment-salvation prophecy, the evidence that its speaker stood in the line of Israelitic prophetic function, its treatment of themes common to Israelitic liturgy and theology, its evidence of authentic roots in Israelitic prophetic tra-

---

95. *Ibid.*
96. Cf. the survey of the problem and pertinent literature in *Vision and Prophecy*, chap. 1.
97. Cf. Jer. 49 : 14–16, 9 and Obad. 1b–5, and the comparison on pp. 31f.

dition, and its relevance to problems of faith in its time and afterwards.

D. OBADIAH IN ISRAEL'S WORSHIP

A cardinal rule of exegesis has been to interpret 'in context.' This presupposes a literary frame of reference. But what is the context of a little prophecy like Obadiah? The prophecies around it in the Book of the Twelve are not its proper context. They can, at best, furnish parallels for comparison. Yet the basic need to gain perspective from a larger frame of reference remains. No words, speeches, or writings can be understood without it.

The discipline of form criticism has moved to fill the gap by seeking the *Sitz im Leben* or 'place in life' in which these words were spoken and in which they were originally at home. This presumes that these oracles were presented orally on a particular occasion to fill a specific function within a prescribed setting. The key to this setting or 'context in life' lies in the 'form' of our recorded material and the hints it gives of the setting in which it received this 'form.' The themes, the order in which they were presented, set phrases, and hints at liturgical proceedings help to classify the prophecy. Comparison with other passages may establish parallels, and a group of such parallel and similar passages may be classified as a distinct 'form.' It has been established that such distinct forms tend to have had the same or similar functions and settings. That is, they presuppose a similar 'context in life.'

It is natural to suppose that religious literature would originate from a religious setting. So one seeks the place in worship and tries to establish this place with what goes before and after it as exactly as possible.

Recent studies have established that the prophet played an essential role in Israel's worship alongside the priest. Israel's worship made room for the immediate and pertinent 'word of the Lord' as well as for the traditions of his 'mighty acts,' which expressed his will. The prophets were the bearers of this 'word of the Lord.'

The 'word' came in many forms. Some of them are determined by the content; some by aesthetic or formal considerations; and some by the function the 'word' is to fill in the worship service.

Most prophetic forms are determined by a combination of these factors.

Obadiah has the form of a liturgical foreign prophecy of judgment composed of several units. It obviously fits into the broader theme of the Day of Jahweh. It was directed against Edom. Historical considerations have established a date at the end of the sixth or the first half of the fifth century BC. The geographical location is apparently Jerusalem.

Classical prophecy of this type arose in pre-exilic Judah and Israel in close connection with royal festivals at such places as Bethel and Jerusalem. The festival has been given many names, including that of 'the New Year,' and has been broadly described. Particularly the *Sitz im Leben* of prophecies of judgment and of judgment against foreign nations has been fixed. The celebration of the reign of Jahweh in the heavens and the earth, over Israel and the nations, was related to the confirmation of the Davidic king on his throne as vice-regent for God in his rule over Israel and the nations. This latter phase took the form of covenant renewal.

What form the festival took after the Exile is not clear. The preservation of Psalms from the pre-exilic festival in the Psalter testify to their continued use. But the way they were used may have been very different. Postexilic prophecy held to the central themes of the reign of Jahweh, the expectation of his Day as a day of judgment and salvation, and the reiteration of the messianic promises to David. Yet many elements must have been changed substantially. Some help in reconstructing the festival may be gained from Haggai and the early chapters of Zechariah, which reflect conditions in Jerusalem some years before Obadiah, and from Ezra-Nehemiah, which reflect the period shortly after.

The theme of the early portions of the festival may well have been the same as those in pre-exilic times: the celebration of the reign of Jahweh in heaven and on earth. The royal features of the latter portions must have fallen into the background or simply been absorbed as a portion of the 'restoration of Israel' theme. Certainly the current situation of a scattered and dispersed people was never lost to view.

The obvious discrepancy between the promises to David and present conditions give the tragic background for the festival. The many ways in which Israel's neighbors actively opposed her every effort at reconstruction add a note of poignant relevance to the theme. Both of these factors in the rather drab existence which was Jerusalem's in that time put faith to a fearful test. The theme of the festival celebrated the glorious and sovereign Jahweh who had chosen Israel as his own people. But the harsh reality of everyday experience was that of a dispossessed people cowering on a pile of rubbish which was once David's city but now did not even have a wall. Open to raids from every passing band of vandals, not daring any step which might displease her neighbors, grubbing a bare existence out of the rocky soil, Jerusalem showed no sign of being the Zion of the Psalms, the city of God and the seat of his authority and majesty.

After the festal proclamations of Jahweh's power and rule came the announcement of his day of judgment over Israel and over the nations. He sat in judgment with Israel concerning her loyalty to the covenant, but from the nations he demanded recognition of his own authority. The test of their relation to Jahweh was their attitude and acts toward Jahweh's king, his city, and his people.

This is the *Sitz im Leben* of the foreign prophecies as it is for the prophecies of judgment as a whole. Before Jahweh's reigning and judging presence both Israel and the nations had to appear. Obadiah presents the prophetic introduction of one scene in that great drama of judgment.

The judgment takes place on the Day of Jahweh. Whether that is thought of as actually happening in the festal ritual or whether it only pictures what is understood to happen at some future time can never be determined with absolute clarity. It is likely that such a dramatic ritual was thoroughly capable of ambivalent interpretation in which both were present. The heavy emphasis on the real presence of Jahweh in Jerusalem during the ritual warns against dismissing the sense of present sentence and judgment too lightly. The way in which Israel throughout her history showed herself capable and willing to wait for realistic historic fulfillment of that which was so vividly promised in her worship warns against dismissing the future orientation too lightly. The festival brought creation down into the present. It made the great facts of past history contemporaneous. It also made the consummation of the promise a living reality for faith. All this because of the living presence of the Lord who is 'the same yesterday, today, and forever.'

Note, however, that the Day of Jahweh is viewed as very near. It is announced as the imminent, not far-off, consummation of history. The climactic day of the festival was that day, whether it was thought of realistically or as foreshadowing a reality yet to come. Israel and the peoples are summoned to repentance and faith with the announcement of its coming. No timetable of intervening events is given such as is found in later apocalyptic writing. The emphasis is rather on the call to faith *now,* for the messengers of judgment have already been sent out.

E. THE THEOLOGICAL BACKGROUND

In trying to gain an orientation of Obadiah's place in the development of Old Testament theology one needs to keep in mind that Obadiah comes between Haggai-Zechariah's Jerusalem of 516 BC and Ezra-Nehemiah's reforms of the second half of the fifth century.

The struggle reflected in the former to form their faith anew in the midst of very changed circumstances, was still going on. They were familiar with the great literature which had been current for the exiles. Deuteronomy and the Deuteronomic history still helped to explain God's total purpose and the reasons for judgment that sent Israel and Judah into exile. The great pre-exilic prophets, along with Ezekiel and Deutero-Isaiah from the Exile, would have been well known. Jerusalem was probably not yet impressed by the resurgence of priestly theology that was already influential in Babylon and would shortly be brought back to Jerusalem by Ezra.

Both Ezekiel and Deutero-Isaiah had prepared for the return to Canaan with great fanfare. The return to Jerusalem was announced in terms that signaled the beginning of the Messianic Age. But those who actually made the trip were terribly disillusioned and discouraged by the time Haggai and Zechariah prophesied. The rebuilt Temple apparently did little to remedy the situation, and morale in Obadiah's time could hardly have been better than before. The problem of leadership had become even more acute. Thus, for those whose faith was bolstered by messianic promises to David, the times were of acute crisis. Zion was a ruin ruled by a distant Persian tyrant and harassed by jealous neighbors. None of the line of David had led the people since Zerubbabel, and there appeared little chance of finding another in the near future.

Ancient Israelitic faith had clung to the promise made to Abraham that the land would belong to his seed. Deuteronomy had made much of the possession of the land as a ground for faith and a goal for Israel's history. The return from Babylon must have rekindled such faith in many a pilgrim's heart. But the situation a half-century later was one of a very precarious hold on Judaea under extreme pressure from several sides. This could not be understood as the fulfillment of the promise to Abraham, and Abraham's children were discouraged and resentful.

Israel had been proud of being the people of Jahweh. They gathered as one people to show their unity under his leadership. After the division of the kingdoms and the scattering into exile, a frequently heard feature of hope lay in gathering the people together again as one people. But the realistic situation in this respect was equally depressing. Exiles from the Assyrian invasions were so thoroughly scattered across the upper Mesopotamian valley and even Asia Minor that they could hardly be indentified. Judaean exiles populated many communities in lower Mesopotamia as well as Egypt and even North Africa. As refugees they continued to exist for one generation after another.

Under such conditions where should one look for God, for evidence of his purpose and reign, of his justice and retribution against evil, of his salvation and gracious will for his own people? For such a time Obadiah speaks a word intended to clear the vision and uphold the heart. His faith never wavers from the assurance of Jahweh's nearness and reigning power. He is sure of his justice and that he will certainly attain his goal.

II
THE TEXT OF OBADIAH

A. INTRODUCTION TO THE TEXT

The exegete's first task is always that of text criticism. It is sometimes a difficult and annoying task, requiring great attention to detail, but it is unavoidable. If its problems are not settled before beginning interpretation, a great deal of mischief can be done. For then one is tempted to shape the text in accord with inclinations of interpretation rather than on strict text-critical principles.

In order to keep this position primary a full consonantal text is printed here. It is an emended text showing the form that will actually be the basis for the commentary. It will be well for the reader to keep a critical edition of the Hebrew Bible at hand for comparison. The basis and reasons for any change in the text will be carefully noted.

The text is printed in a form that will demonstrate the metrical arrangement of the words. The MT had long since lost this consciousness of poetry and meter that is inherent in most prophetic speech. This very failure to recognize it as poetry has sometimes led to errors in textual transmission. Meter can sometimes be a help in correcting the text, although it is not an absolute criterion. But recognition of the metrical form is important to the interpreter as well. It often is an aid in determining the proper divisions of the text, in helping to catch the mood of the passage, and in showing the proper logical or aesthetic relation of phrases and lines.

Scholars are not in agreement concerning many aspects of Hebrew poetry and meter. But the basic ideas are fairly generally accepted and are applied here. The fundamental idea is that of parallelism. Lines or stichoi are parallel in thought and/or form to other lines or stichoi. A line of poetry is composed of two or three stichoi. Each stichos has two, three, or four accents – usually one to a word. The system pays no heed to the number of syllables and makes no systematic use of rhyme. Strophes can be found, but there is no agreement on principles of strophic form. Apparently such formation followed no set rules. The verse numbers and divisions now found in the Bible are often of no help in determining line or strophic divisions. They should be ignored.

For purposes of convenience, meter has been indicated by numbers in the right margin. They are to be read from right to left like the Hebrew text. It will be obvious that the most common forms are in 3–3 or 2–3 meter. This is also true in Hebrew poetry generally.

Some words, adverbs or conjunctions, and even some phrases, are put outside the metrical structure and called 'anacrusis.' It may be that these were actually spoken in the text from the beginning. But it is highly likely that the transmission of the text has tended to increase the use of such words. Some students of old Hebrew poetry insist that it originally had neither articles nor conjunctions and, therefore, eliminate them consistently from the Textus Receptus of such poetry to arrive at the original form of these poems. This has not been done in this text. But such obvious words as הנה and כִּי, as well as the introductory and concluding phrases for oracles, have been set outside the metrical pattern.

The text of Obadiah is generally in very good shape and can be treated simply by notes under the text. But one item may best be treated in detail separately. There is a remarkable parallel to Obadiah 1b–4 in Jeremiah 49:14–16 and between Obadiah 5 and Jeremiah 49:9. This calls for explanation and treatment. The questions of originality and source will be treated in the commentary. Here they will be compared from a text-critical view to determine whether the text of Jeremiah can be of help in studying the text of Obadiah.[1]

Here are the texts placed side by side:

1. Cf. H. Bekel, 'Ein vorexilisches Orakel über Edom in der Klagestrophe – die gemeinsame Quelle von Obadja 1–9 und Jeremia 49 : 7–22,' *Theologische Studien und Kritiken*, 80 (1907), 315–343. T. H. Robinson, 'The Structure of the Book of Obadiah,' *Journal of Theological Studies*, XVII (1916), 402–408.

B. COMPARISON OF THE TEXTS: OBADIAH 1b–5 AND JEREMIAH 49:14–16, 9

שמועה שמענו מאת־יהוה וציר בגוים שלח	3‑3	1b
שמועה שמעתי מאת־יהוה וציר בגוים שלוח	3‑3	49:14a
קומו ונקומה עליה למלחמה	1‑3	1c
התקבצו ובאו עליה וקומו למלחמה	2‑3	49:14b
הנה) קטן נתתיך בגוים בזוי אתה מאד	3‑3	2
כי הנה) קטן נתתיך בגוים בזוי באדם	2‑3	49:15
זדון לבך השיאך	3	3a
תפלצתך השיא אתך זדון לבך	2‑3	49:16a
שכני בחגוי סלע מרום שבתו	2‑3	3b
שכני בחגוי הסלע תפשי מרום גבעה	3‑3	49:16b
אמר בלבו מי יורדני ארץ	3‑2	3c
אם תגביה כנשר ואם שׂם כוכבים שים קנך משם אורידך	2‑5‑3	4a
כי תגביה כנשר קנך משם אורידך	2‑2‑2	49:16c
נאם יהוה		4b
נאם יהוה		49:16d
אם גנבים באו לך אם שודדי לילה		5a
אם גנבים בלילה		49:9ba
איך נדמיתה הלוא יגבו דים		5b
השחיתו דים		49:9bb
אם בצרים באו לך הלוא ישאירו עללות		5c
אם בצרים באו לך לא ישאירו עוללות		49:9a

The similarity is striking – so much so as to tempt one to postulate identity. Even the differences often show different combinations of the same orthographic elements and thus due to corruption in transmission rather than a different source.

The first lines (Obad. 1a – Jer. 49:14a) are virtually identical. The first stichos is first person plural in Obadiah and singular in Jeremiah. The last words differ in that there is one additional vowel letter in Jeremiah, causing it to be pointed as a Qal passive participle rather than a Pu'al perfect. But the meaning of the two does not vary significantly. The meter of both is good.

The second lines vary more. Obadiah 1c is metrically difficult (1–3) and duplicates its one verb in two forms, which though grammatically possible is stylistically awkward. Jeremiah 49:14b has better meter (2–3) and avoids the duplication of verb root. But it includes all three other words of the Obadiah text, though in a slightly different order. The meaning of the two is similar, but Jeremiah's text is structurally sounder. Their identity is clear, but Obadiah gives the appearance of a text that was corrupted and then reconstructed.

The third lines, after eliminating the anacrusis in each, yield identical readings except at the end. Metrically either reading is sound. Again it is interesting to find the last three letters identical but differently arranged. It can hardly be doubted that they are different renderings of the same original. There is no significant difference in meaning in the two lines. The Jeremiah reading may be preferred as somewhat better.

The fourth line (Obad. 3a – Jer. 49:16a) is a single stichos of three words in Obadiah. Jeremiah has a full line in 2–3 measure with one more word and the separate reading of a pronominal suffix. The other three words are identical but in a different order. Jeremiah's reading is to be preferred on the grounds of meter only.

The fifth line (Obad. 3b – Jer. 49:16b) has good reading and meter in Obadiah. Jeremiah adds an article and one word and has a different word at the end. Obadiah's text is sound and appears more original.

The sixth line (Obad. 3c) has no parallel in Jeremiah. Although it reverses the metrical balance (3–2 instead of the usual 2–3) it fits well and may be kept.

The seventh line (Obad. 4a – Jer. 49:16a) has five words identical. The opening words differ, but are simply synonyms. But Obadiah has a whole extra phrase of four words. These overload the meter beyond endurance. They add to the meaning only in increasing the contrast in the comparison. This is an example of a typical gloss, which creeps into the text from a devotional comment that some scribe originally put in the margin. The oracle loses nothing by eliminating the words, while it certainly gains in metrical clarity and poetic compactness. So the Jeremiah form is to be preferred.

Both versions end here with the closing formula for an oracle.

Obadiah's second oracle begins with a verse (v. 5) that also has a parallel in Jeremiah's oracle against Edom (Jer. 49:9). Jeremiah's version is shorter and presents the two statements in reverse order. The Obadiah text presents problems of meaning, for the additional phrase anticipates verse 6 and destroys the obviously intended contrast. The Jeremiah text is used to reorder the lines, with the additional portion placed as the third of three lines that can be paired with verse 6 (see the emended text below).

This comparison shows that the two texts must have a single source. Differences are of the kind that come in transmission rather than original composition. T. H. Robinson's judgment that the material is more original in Obadiah, but better preserved in Jeremiah, can hardly be improved upon. This presumes that both drew on a common source that was older than either. On this view it should be legitimate to use Jeremiah as a basis for emending the Obadiah text at those points where some correction seems necessary.

C. THE HEBREW TEXT

The text of Obadiah, with corrections and rearrangements where it has been deemed necessary, follows. Footnotes document the reason for every variation from the Ben Asher text printed in Kittel's seventh edition. The metrical notations read from right to left.

חזון עבדיה   1

שמועה שמענו מאת־יהוה   וציר בגוים שלח   3–3
התקבצו ובאו עליה^a   וקומו למלחמה   2–3

כה אמר אדני יהוה לאדום^b
הנה^c   2
קטן נתתיך בגוים   בזוי באדם^d   2–3
תפלצתך השיא אתך^e   3   זדון לבך   2–3
שכני בחגוי סלע   מרום שבתו   2–3
אמר בלבו   מי יורדני ארץ   3–2
אם תגביה כנשר^f   קנך   משם אורידך   4   2–2–2
נאם יהוה
אם בצרים באו־לך^g   5   הלא ישאירו עללות   3–3
אם גנבים ^hבלילה   הלוא יגנבו דים   3–3
ואם שדדים ^hבאו־לך   איך נדמיתה   2–3
איך נחפשו עשו   6   נבעו מצפניו   2–3
עד הגבול שלחוך   7   כל אנשי בריתך השיאוך   4–3
יכלו לך אנשי שלמך   ישימו מזור תחתיך^i   3–4
אין תבונה בו :   8   הלוא ביום ההוא^j   3–3
והאבדתי חכמים מאדום   ותבונה מהר עשו   3–3

---

a. The parallel line in Jer. 49 : 14 is better metrically and apparently more original than the קומו ונקומה עליה למלחמה of Obad.

b. This is a formal introduction to direct speech, out of place in v. 1, but fitting perfectly before v. 2. (See discussion under 'Form.')

c. Anacrusis – outside the metrical arrangement.

d. Emended acc. to Jer. 49 : 15 instead of אתה מאד. Letters similar but rearranged.

e. The line from Jer. 49 : 16a has been substituted for Obad. 3a, which is metrically faulty: זדון לבך השיאך

f. ואם־בין כוכבים שים omitted as a gloss. If it were kept it should form a separate line. But it is better to omit it with Jer. 49 : 16b.

g. The two lines of v. 5 have been reversed as Jer. 49 : 9.

h. באו־לך and איך נמיתה – אם־שודדי have been dropped to the next line. They anticipate v. 6 in tone and content and break the relation between the parts of v. 5. Then לילה is written with ב, following the text in Jeremiah.

i. לחמך – is deleted as a reduplication of sense. See LXX.

j. נאם־יהוה – is placed at the end of the oracle, v. 10, the normal place for such a phrase.

וחתו גבוריך תימן למען יכרת איש מהר עשו מקטלᵃ 9 3–3–3

מחמס אחיך יעקב תכסך בושה ונכרת לעולם 10 2–2–3
ⁿאם יהוה

ביום עמדך מנגד ביום שבות זרים חילו 11 3–4
ונכרים באו שערו ועל־ירושלם ידו גורל גם־אתה 3–3–3
כאחד מהם

ואל־תרא ביום אחיך ביום נכרו 12 2–3
ואל־תשמח לבני יהודה ביום אבדם 2–3
ואל־תגדל פיך ביום צרה 2–2

אל־תבוא בשער עמי ביום אידם 13 2–3
אל־תרא גם־אתה ברעתו ביום אידו 2–3
ואל־תשלח ˡיד בחילו ביום ᵐאבדו 2–3

ואל־תעמד על־הפרק להכרית את־פליטיו 14 2–2
ואל־תסגר שרידיו ביום צרה 2–2

ⁿכי) קרוב יום יהוה על־כל הגוים 15 2–3
כאשר עשית יעשה לך גמלך ישוב בראשך 3–2–2

ⁿכי) כאשר שתיתם על־הר קדשי ישתו 16 3–2–2
כל־הגוים תמידᵒ
ושתו ולעו והיו כלוא היו 3–2

ובהר ציון תהיה פליטה והיה קדש 17 2–2–2
וירשו בית יעקב את מורשיהם 2–3

והיה בית־יעקב אש ובית יוסף להבה ובית עשו 18 3–3–3
לקש
ודלקו בהם ואכלום ולא יהוה שריד לבית עשו 3–3–3
כי יהוה דבר

וירשו הנגב את־הר עשו והשפלה ᵖאת־שדה אפריםᑫ 19 2–3–4
ובנימן את־הגלעד

k. Retained, although it has often been called a gloss. It fits metrically
and makes sense.

l. Emendation of נה to יד. The person is grammatically inappropriate.
The change is orthographically understandable.

m. Following the LXX: ἀπωλίας – אבדו – 'destruction.'

n. Anacrusis. It falls outside the metrical structure.

o. Some manuscripts: סביב; LXX AQN א c a οἶνον – חמר – 'wine';
LXXᴮ omits. None of these is better than the MT. Let it stand.

p. Omit את־פלשתים – a corruption of the word before it and disturbs
the meter. The sense of the passage is not changed. Also omit וירשו as
a filler inserted after the other word had entered the text.

q. Omit ואת־שמרון as a gloss on 'The field of Ephraim.'

20   וגלת ׳בחלה לבני ישראל ירשו ארץˢ כנענים
עד־צרפת
וגלת ירושלם אשר בספרד   ירשו את ערי הנגב
21 ועלו משעים בהר ציון   לשפט את־הר עשו
והיתה ליהוה המלוכה

r. Emendation for החיל־הזה – following Oort and Robinson. See LXX. It adds to the sense and is parallel to the next line.

s. Instead of אשר, which is judged a corruption and does not make sense.

III
A DISTINCTIVE
TRANSLATION OF
OBADIAH

A. INTRODUCTION TO THE TRANSLATION

The translation that follows attempts to convey the distinctive connotations of Hebrew word meanings, grammatical forms, and syntactical arrangements. Stylistic shadings will also be noted to the extent that translation allows. To do this, the principles suggested in my father's book on syntax[1] and already applied by him to the translation of the book of Genesis[2] will be used.

The Hebrew meter will be noted in the left margin, with numbers reading from left to right to match the translated text. Separate stichoi will be indicated by separate lines in the translation, with second and third stichoi indented.

Hebrew tenses do not designate time. The time viewpoint must be determined from the context before the various verb forms can be correctly translated. The time viewpoint of each passage is, therefore, noted in the left margin.

In order to locate precisely the syntactical form of each verb and subordinate clause small numbers have been inserted in the translation. They refer to the key in J. Wash Watts, *Syntax,* 1st ed., pp. 120–121, and are primarily intended for the student who wishes to check the reasons why particular translations have been chosen in each instance.[3] In general use they can be safely ignored.

1. J. Wash Watts, *A Survey of Syntax in the Hebrew Old Testament,* rev. ed. (Grand Rapids, 1964).
2. J. Wash Watts, *A Distinctive Translation of Genesis* (Grand Rapids, 1963).
3. Since this summary has been eliminated from the second edition, the list of abbreviations used in this translation with identifying numbers is repeated:
  1. narrative perfect
  2. emphatic perfect

Hebrew uses a changed word-order to achieve particular emphasis. This is not always obvious in an English translation. Such emphases are there marked by italicizing the emphasized word in the English translation.

B. A DISTINCTIVE TRANSLATION OF OBADIAH

(Numbers in text identify syntactical forms listed in footnote 3.)

1. The vision of Jahweh's Servant.

present

        An audition we have heard[5] from Jahweh

3–3   that an envoy has been sent[5] among the nations:

future   'Assemble yourselves[24] and come[24] against her.

3–2   Rise up[24] for the battle.'

present   Thus says[2] the Lord Jahweh to Edom:

future   2. 'Behold,

          small will I make[4] you among the nations,

3–2   despised among mankind.

        3. Your '*Horror*' shall deceive[4] you,

3–2   the presumptuousness of your heart,

          O dweller[15] in sanctuaries of rock,

3. perfect of confidence
4. prophetic perfect
5. present perfect
6. characteristic perfect
7. correlative perfect
9. progressive imperfect
10. characteristic imperfect
15. active participle used as noun or adjective
19. contrary-to-fact subjunctive
20. potential subjunctive
22. optative subjunctive
24. imperative imperfect
32. infinitive construct + ל (purpose or result)
43. verb 'to be' understood
46. relative clause
52. condition taken for granted
55. less probable condition

3–2	whose[46] home is[43] high,
	saying[15] in his heart,
2–3	'Who can bring me down[20] to earth?'
	4. Though[55] you should raise[20]
	your nest like the eagle,
2–2–2	from thence I would pull[20] you down.'
	Expression of Jahweh.

present	5. If[52] grape-gatherers come[6] to you,
3–3	do they not customarily leave[10] gleanings?
	If[52] thieves in the night,
3–3	do they not usually steal[10] their sufficiency?
	(what they need)
future	But if[52] plunderers shall come[3] to you,
3–2	how you shall be destroyed![4]
	6. How Esau shall be searched out![4]
3–2	his hidden treasures sought out![4]
	7. To the border shall they send you.[4]
3–4	All the men of your covenant shall deceive[4] you.
	Men of your alliance shall gain power[4] over you
4–3	(in that) they will move to set[9] a trap under you.
	(Although) there will be[43] no apprehension of it,
3–3	8. will it not be[43] in that day
	that I will destroy[7] wise ones from Edom
3–3	and understanding from the mountain of Esau;
	9. that your heroes shall be shattered,[7] Teman,
	so that to a man they will be cut off[9]
3–3–3	from the mountain of Esau by slaɔghter?
	10. On account of violence (toward) your brother Jacob
	shame will proceed to cover[9] you,
3–2–2	and you shall be cut off[7] forever.
	Expression of Jahweh.

past	11. In the day that you stood[32] aloof,
3–4	in the day that foreigners captured[32] his
	fortifications,
	when *strangers* entered[1] his gates,
	and *for Jerusalem* they cast[1] lots,

3–3–3   even *you* were[43] like one of them.

  12. But you should never look[22] on the day of your brother

3–2   in the day of his calamity,

      nor rejoice[22] over Judaeans

3–2   in the day of their destruction,

      nor stretch[22] your mouth

2–2   on the day of distress.

  13. You should never enter[22] the gate of my people

3–2   on the day of their calamity.

      You should never look,[22] especially you, on his ill fortune

3–2   on the day of his calamity,

      nor stretch out[22] a hand among his goods

3–2   on the day of his destruction,

  14. nor stand[22] on the crossing

2–2   to cut off[35] his refugees,

      nor imprison[22] his survivors

2–2   on the day of distress.

present   15. For

      the Day of Jahweh is[43] near

3–2   upon all the nations.

      As you have done,[5]

      it will proceed to be done[9] to you.

2–2–3   *Your dealing* will return[9] on your head.

  16. For

      s you have drunk[5]

      on the mount of my holiness,

2–2–3   will all the nations drink[9] continuously,

      and they shall drink[7] and blabber drunkenly,[7]

2–3   and become[7] as though they do not exist.[19]

future   17. But *in Mount Zion*

      there will continue to be[9] an escaped remnant,

2–2–2   and it shall be[7] a holy one.

      And the House of Jacob shall possess[7]

3–2   their possession.

40

18. And the House of Jacob shall be[7] fire,
        and the House of Joseph a flame,
3–3–3   but the House of Esau chaff.
    They shall burn[7] them and devour[7] them,
        nor will a survivor remain[9]
3–3–2   to the House of Esau.
present   For Jahweh has spoken.[5]
future 19. They of the Negeb shall possess[7] the mountain of
                                    Esau,
        and they of the Shephelah the field of Ephraim,
4–3–2   and Benjamin, Gilead.
    20. The exiles of Israelites in Chalah
4–4   shall possess[4] the Canaanites' land as far as
                                    Zaraphath.
    The exiles of Jerusalem who are[43] in Sepharad
4–4   shall possess[4] the villages of the Negeb.
4–3–3 21. Saviors shall rise[7] in Mount Zion
        to judge[35] the mountain of Esau,
        and dominion shall belong[7] to Jahweh.

IV

COMMENTARY

A. THE SUPERSCRIPTION (V. 1a)

'The vision of' is a common element in the titles of prophetic books or oracles and is found also in Isaiah 1:1 and Nahum 1:1. It refers to the product of ecstatic inspiration by which Jahweh revealed his will through the prophets. It is parallel to 'the word' received by the prophet, and the concepts are often interchanged as in Amos 1:1.

The vision is to be sharply differentiated from common sight and things seen. It is the result of inspiration and is understood as having unique significance since it is given by God himself. The common word for seeing can be applied to what is seen in a vision (Amos 7), but the visionary experience implies insight and perception as well as simply seeing. This word is, therefore, reserved for this deeper and more specialized meaning.

In Hebrew prophecy a vision is simply a medium for the communication of a 'word' from Jahweh. Therefore, many books with this title contain little else than 'words' or speeches. This is also true here. The contents of this first verse might properly be called a vision, for apparently the messenger or his errand was seen. But it is actually called 'an audition.' In a vision the prophet actually sees and hears. What he sees helps him to understand what he hears.

In titles of this kind a proper name is regularly mentioned. It is in the genitive case: Isaiah's or Nahum's or Obadiah's vision. It is clear that prophetic vision is not a general broadcast from heaven that happens to be picked up by any particularly sensitive antenna. It was directed to a particular person who was then responsible for it. This is in the very nature of prophecy itself. It is not naturally anonymous.

Yet the fact remains that several prophets remain nameless in the Old Testament (I Kings 13; 20:3; and others), and in many other instances research has established that much prophetic material in the Old Testament was not actually composed by known prophets (e.g., Isa. 40ff.). In many instances nothing is known of a prophet except that which appears in his book (e.g., Amos, Hos., Ezek.). Some of these are at pains to include biographical material, clearly stressing the importance of recognizing the individual personality of the man who mediates God's word to Israel (Amos 1:1; 7:10–17; passages in Isa. and Jer.). Some others have nothing more than the name (Hab. and Mal.). In one or two instances the names are such as to suggest that they are merely titles, indicating that the actual names of the prophets were unknown to the compilers or were considered unimportant.[1]

Obadiah is a name found a number of times in the Old Testament.[2] Earlier it had been written עֹבַדְיָהוּ. In this form it appears three times of persons living before the Exile (I Kings 18:3–7; I Chron. 27:19; II Chron. 34:12). The shorter form, like that of the prophet, is recorded for several Jews returning from exile (Ezra 8:9; Neh. 10:6; 12:25. Perhaps also Neh. 11:17 // to I Chron. 9:16. Cf. also I Chron. 8:38; 9:44; 3:21; 8:3; 12:9; II Chron. 17:7). The Massoretic pointing עֹבַדְיָה suggests the translation 'worshipper of Jahweh.'[3] But the transliteration of several Greek versions[4] suggests the pointing עֶבֶד יָה: 'Servant of Jahweh.'

The name has possibilities of meaning which are at the same time commonplace and deeply meaningful. The people of the Near East were accustomed to theophoric names, a habit for which the archaeologist and historian of religion are very thankful. One of the most common of all was that which simply identified a man as a devotee of such and such a God. Such names compounded with Ba'al and 'El as well as with Jahweh or its abbreviations are common in the Old Testament.

The other possibility must not be left out, however. In the royal devotional thought and ritual of the Davidic house the term 'Servant of Jahweh' had always had a special meaning for the king. Isaiah 42, 49, 51, and 53 had applied the term in a manner that no

1. Malachi means 'my messenger' and as such appears in Mal. 3 : 1.
2. Cf. the extensive treatment of G. A. Smith, *op. cit.*, p. 163; and Eiselen, II, 431, n. 431.
3. Supported by LXX[B] – 'Οβδειού.
4. L, A, Th and א – 'Αβδιού or 'Αβδειού.

future generations could ignore.

The wide spectrum of possible meaning in the name is apparent. But a more critical question is posed: Is the term an actual proper name? Or is it simply a kind of title symbolic of the prophetic office substituted where no name was actually known? The possibility of the former is clear from the parallels that have been cited of men who were undoubtedly called by this name. But lack of more exact identification in terms of genealogy, home, or date means that the latter cannot be ruled out. Perhaps the very liturgical character of the book, drawing heavily upon traditional prophetic material as it does, made it more appropriate to use a general term than a proper name.

Such a title was obviously the work of a compiler or editor. It belongs to the literary edition rather than the spoken prophecy. The phrase that follows, 'Thus says the Lord Jahweh to Edom,' should by its nature be a part of an oracle spoken in the first person for Jahweh. In terms of that function, it is obviously out of place here. No oracle follows, but a vision or audition. The first person speech is not Jahweh's but the prophet's.

Apparently the original place of the introductory phrase would properly be before verse 2, where it would fit beautifully. The emended text and translation have already placed it there, and the commentary will deal with it more fully at that place.

This means that an editor or compiler has moved it to its present location as part of the heading for the book. Why should he have felt that necessary? What was accomplished by doing that? Two answers may be proposed. One obvious suggestion is that it serves to identify the entire book as a prophecy against Edom. This would make it into a parallel to the heading of so many foreign prophecies.

The second suggestion may be more to the point. The literary compilation of prophecy had at an early date fixed certain stereotyped forms by which true prophecy could be recognized. One of these was the introductory formula which appears before many oracles, 'Thus says Jahweh.' A prophetic liturgy like Obadiah was identified in its actual rendition by the position it took in the broader liturgy of festival or worship and by its speaker. These were lacking in its literary form. At first glance it might not have

been recognized as a prophecy at all. By moving this typical proph
etic formula to support the actual title of the book, the compiler
guaranteed its easy recognition as prophecy and its theme as *con-
tra* Edom.

B. THE AUDITION (V. 1b–c)

In both form and function the narration of such a prophetic
experience must be distinguished from an oracle or 'word.' It
related something heard or seen in ecstatic prophetic experience. It
may recount simply a normal event which has received heightened
significance by being pointed out to the prophet by Jahweh, or it
may be a completely visionary experience which has no relation to
natural things or events.

It is usually cryptic in meaning, as here, simply giving a focus or
point of departure for the speeches that follow. Its purpose is to
authenticate the divine origin of the messages and to document
the way in which God brought the prophet's attention to bear on
this particular issue.

The prophet has received certain tidings or news. He is con-
vinced that it has been brought to his attention by Jahweh. The
prophet is, therefore, being challenged to look for the deeper
meaning, to search out the relevance of this event to the work of
Jahweh in history and with Israel.

The contents of the news or rumor are simple: a messenger or
envoy has been sent to call the nations to war against a third party
which is not identified. The news does not say that Jahweh sent
the envoy. The implication is that some nation is summoning the
others to join it in an invasion. Jahweh simply calls the prophet's
attention to the news.

The audition is cryptic in the extreme and cries out for explanation and clarification. It serves admirably as an introduction to
what follows. Jahweh has called the attention of prophet and people to news of preparation for war. He implies that this is his doing
and that the outcome is of special significance for the people of
God.

If the *Sitz im Leben* has been properly located, the festival con-
gregation had already celebrated Jahweh's eternal reign in Jeru-

salem. They now turn their attention toward the renewal of the covenant. At that point Jahweh sits in judgment over Israel and the nations. As part of this judgment procedure, prophets speak out against one and then another. The festival has stressed the abiding truths inherent in their understanding of Jahweh's reign: his creation of the world, his control of nature, his actions in history that called Israel into existence, etc. In the judgment phase attention is drawn to the present. The distinctive prophetic task was to interpret God's will for the now and the future. God's action in current events is their theme. To evoke obedient faith and understanding from the people as they faced these events was their aim.

With the recital of this experience of audition Obadiah begins his address to the people. He brings a 'rumor of war' which Jahweh had called to his attention and, by implication, had instructed him to interpret to the people.

C. THE FIRST ANNOUNCEMENT OF JUDGMENT (VV. 2–4)

	lab. Thus says[2] the Lord Jahweh to Edom:
	2. Behold,
	small will I make[4] you among the nations,
3–2	despised among mankind.
	3. Your *'Horror'* shall deceive[4] you,
3–2	the presumptuousness of your heart,
	O dweller[15] in sanctuaries of rock,
3–2	whose[46] home is[43] high,
	saying[15] in his heart,
2–3	'Who can bring me down[20] to earth?'
	4. Though[55] you should raise[20]
	your nest like the eagle,
2–2–2	from thence I would pull you down.'[20]
	Expression of Jahweh.

The oracle takes the form of a Jahweh-word with its introductory 'Thus says Jahweh' and concluding 'Expression of Jahweh.' It includes 4 lines in predominant *qinah* or 3–2 measure. This gives it the tone of a dirge. It concludes with a tristich 2–2–2 line which broadens its tone and emphasizes the announcement of doom.

The introduction has been moved from its position in the superscription in the MT where it introduces nothing. Here it is naturally at home and fills out the form of the passage. The simple form, 'Thus says Jahweh,' is the most common formula in prophecy for the introduction of a prophetic oracle. The words are to be understood as a message being delivered orally by a messenger. The prophet was the messenger. But the sender was none other than Jahweh himself.

The use of the sacred name emphasized that the message is set within the context of the God-man relation that was defined by the covenant with Israel. Jahweh was the distinctive covenant name for God which was revealed to Israel in the complex of events that created the covenant. It was proclaimed, worshipped, and continued in covenant-renewal ceremonies. Here oracles of judgment, such as this, were also at home. Jahweh, the God of covenant, speaks.

The use of the double name, Lord Jahweh, is infrequent enough to deserve comment. Amos was one of the first to use the term. For him it comprehended his understanding of Jahweh as Lord of all, of heaven, of earth, of history, of Israel, of himself. It is particularly meaningful when understood in the setting of covenant festival when Jahweh's enthronement as king over heaven and earth has been celebrated and the attention of the celebrants turns to his rule over Israel and all history. Jahweh was truly Lord. This entire prophecy gives one specific example of the exercise of his lordship.

The introduction identifies the receiver as well as the sender of the message. It is addressed 'to Edom.' Whereas the audition had remained cryptic and the victim of the conspiracy unidentified, the Lord's word of prophecy is exactly addressed. Enough has been written in the Introduction about Edom that it will not be necessary to repeat this here. Let it simply be clear that the announcement of the name alone was sufficient to rouse overtones of feeling in Israel which ran deep and were very intense. Edom was a common object of judgment mentioned in the foreign prophecies. Whether other nations were also listed for judgment on this occasion, we cannot know. For the group of oracles are here preserved alone, and all of them are unified in their announcement of doom on Edom.

The announcement turns on three words: 'small,' 'despised,' and 'pulled down.' Edom is to be degraded, dishonored, and laid prostrate. The fact that the judgment emphasizes her relation to other nations is common to the *Sitz im Leben* of foreign prophecy in general. 'The nations' stand for judgment before Jahweh. Their relative positions to each other are at stake. Their actions toward each other often form the basis of judgment.

Using the Jeremiah text has provided a better meter and structure to this verse. It has also introduced a word which is difficult to interpret. תפלצת is a *hapax legomenon* in the Old Testament. One lexicon identifies its root meaning with 'shuddering, horror,'[5] while another suggests 'terror over thee.'[6] Both suggest that it refers here to an idol, perhaps in the form of a phallic image. 'Your horrible idol' is the apparent meaning of the word.

The verse shows a much deeper understanding of the true nature of idolatry, however. The deception that idolatry practices over its adherents is recognized. But it goes even deeper to brand it self-deception. For idols are self-made by the worshippers. The worshippers are not deceived; they deceive themselves. The idol is simply a symbol to which the deepest wishes of the heart attach themselves. So pride and presumption deify themselves in an idol symbol and the cycle of self-deception has run its course. Such self-deception judges itself. Because it keeps the worshipper out of touch with reality, it sets him up for a fall. It robs the practitioner of a realistic estimate of himself or his situation. In that it accomplishes the supreme deception in suggesting that one is not liable to the judgment of God, it guarantees the fall of the worshipper.

Not only Edom's idol, but also her geographical situation has prepared this deception. In the high cliffs of that rocky country cities like Teman and later Petra were built in locations that were virtually impenetrable. The entrances were through tortuous nar-

---

5. *BDB*, p. 814; *K-B*, pp. 746 and 1037: 'the horror caused by thee.'
6. Julius Fürst, *A Hebrew and Chaldee Lexicon to the Old Testament.* 3rd ed. tr. by Samuel Davidson (Leipzig and London, 1867), p. 1487.

row gorges which twisted through the rock, preventing the massing of force at any point. The flanks were protected by unassailable cliffs. Direct attack, even by a much superior force, was unthinkable. So Edom, who lived protected by her high rocky home, considered herself secure, even from Jahweh.

From that high position she looks down on her neighbors and the universe with the thought: 'Who can bring me down to earth?' Jahweh, speaking through his prophet in the great trial scene of covenant judgment, volunteers to answer the unspoken presumption: 'Though you should raise your nest like the eagle, from thence *I* would pull you down.' The syntax is one of a condition contrary to fact – a condition impossible to fulfill; but even there Jahweh's judgment would be effective.

The speech is short and concise, but rich in implication and imagery. It is a worthy example of prophetic oracle. It names the object of judgment, states Jahweh's intention regarding him, and plays poetically on his false faith, his psychological weakness, his characteristic geographical position, and his arrogant attitude.

D. THE SECOND ANNOUNCEMENT OF JUDGMENT (VV. 5–10)

	5. If[52] grape-gatherers come[6] to you,
3–3	do they not customarily leave[10] gleanings?
	If[52] thieves in the night,
3–3	do they not usually steal[10] what they need?
	But if[52] plunderers shall come[3] to you,
3–2	how you shall be destroyed![4]
	6. How Esau shall be searched out![4]
3–2	his hidden treasure sought out![4]
	7. *To the border* shall they send you.[4]
3–4	All the men of your covenant shall deceive you.[4]
	Men of you alliance shall gain power[4] over you
4–3	(in that) they will move to set[9] a trap under you.
	(Although) there will be[43] no apprehension of it,
3–3	8. wil it not be[43] in that day
	that I will destroy[7] wise ones from Edom
3–3	and understanding from the mountain of Esau;

9. that your heroes shall be shattered,[7] Teman,
   so that to a man they will be cut off[9]

3–3–3   from the mountain of Esau by slaughter?

10. On account of violence (toward) your brother Jacob
    shame will proceed to cover[9] you,

3–2–2   and you shall be cut off[7] forever.

Expression of Jahweh.

This message is also a Jahweh-word, but it lacks the opening formula. The 10 lines are neatly grouped in pairs of lines with the 3–3 distich meter dominant. Meter and thematic content vary together.

Two lines in 3–3 meter are questions stating proverbs about light losses. Two lines in *qinah* measure (3–2) lament the much heavier loss that is to be Edom's. Two lines spell out practically in heavier 3–4 and 4–3 measure the treachery that will accomplish this. Two lines return to 3–3 meter and the 'in that day' form to sketch God's action, while two tristich lines in 3–3–3 and 3–2–2 measure indicate the results and the reason for the judgment.

This message expands on both the audition and the first message. It fills in the details of the conspiracy hinted at in the audition and states at the end the crime which necessitates the judgment. Whether it was composed and spoken by the same prophet as the first is uncertain. It would have been for the same occasion, but it is possible that several prophets contributed to the liturgy.

The first lines indicate the grievous nature of the punishment by contrasting it with other things. The grape harvesters cut away the fruit, but they do leave something, if only the hulls of grapes that have yielded up their juice to the press. Thieves that slip into the house at night take only the little things that can be easily carried away. But these will not do for a description of what will happen to Edom.

Her punishment will be like that of a defeated city drunkenly plundered by a conquering army. They steal, and what they cannot steal they ruthlessly destroy. They smash everything in their blind search for something of value, which they know must be there somewhere. Nothing escapes the mixture of wrath and glee that motivates them.

The name Esau is applied.[7] This sets the stage for the deliberate juxtaposition of Esau and Jacob in verses 9–10. It is a name loaded with emotional content. Whether this verse is a play on the way Jacob got the best of his brother in the Genesis narrative is not clear, but it is not impossible.

Then, the means by which the 'dwellers of the rock' are to be degraded and defeated is revealed. Edom's allies[8] will conspire to lure her army away from the rocky retreats to her unprotected borders. There they will spring the trap[9] and overcome her. Then only the rocks will remain, and will be easily overcome since they have been stripped of defenders.

The country's capital is used as an appellative for the whole. Edom is to be 'searched out,' 'sought out,' 'sent out,' 'deceived,' and 'overcome.' Yet the question must certainly arise as to what her noble rulers and defenders will be doing through all this, for she has been a mighty, as well as a proud nation. The answer is given in lines that indicate that they will be completely surprised and unsuspecting. For Jahweh himself will be acting against them 'on that day' of judgment.

Edom had been renowned for its wisdom,[10] and the cunning of its rulers. Yet the prophet confidently predicts that they will have no inkling of the plot. For Jahweh himself will destroy wisdom with the wise from the aptly named 'mountain of Esau.' The disaster that begins with the loss of wisdom will rapidly expand to include a smashed army and a slaughter expected to strip the land of its manhood. The country's capital, Teman, is mentioned as a synonym for the country as a whole.

These descriptions are spoken in terms of predictions, and there

7. Cf. above, p. 12.
8. שָׁלֹם means literally 'welfare, peace.' It may be understood as 'men of your friendship.' In this context the word 'alliance' seems stronger and better. Cf. Isa. 20 : 10; 38 : 22; Ps. 41 : 10.
9. The Hebrew מָזוֹר is a *hapax legomenon* that *BDB* lists as 'very dubious' and Köhler as 'unexplained.' Perhaps it means a 'net,' as 'something extended.' The translation of LXX, Syr, and Vul suggest 'an ambush,' Aq and Th, 'a fetter or bond,' Targ, 'a stumbling block.' Vollers, *ZAW* (1884), p. 16 would emend to מָצוֹד or מְצוֹדָה, meaning 'net.' Prince, *JBL*, XVI (1897), 177 suggests 'siege.'
10. Cf. above, p. 14.

is no reason to presume that they were written *post factum*. Thus it is idle to try to pin down these events in detail.[11] It is not unlikely that the rumor mentioned in the audition did hint at the identity of the allies that were plotting to betray Edom. It may have been the Arabian tribes, who are often thought to have been responsible for her downfall. The worth of the prophecy does not so much lie in such historical details, which are uncertain in any event, but in the judgment that is pronounced and the theological reasons that made it possible and supported it.

The first hint of such theological support comes from the phrase 'in that day.' This reference to the 'Day of Jahweh' confirms the earlier comments concerning the setting of the prophecy. Jahweh is on his judgment throne and is dispensing justice to the nations. Wrongs will be righted, the innocent justified, and the guilty punished.

But the second is a flat statement of the charges against Edom. It is succinctly stated as 'violence (toward) your brother Jacob.' Without elaborating, the line hastens to the punishment: shame and extinction forever. The phrasing is reminiscent of the judgment on Tyre in Amos 1:9. With that the message closes, using the usual formula for a Jahweh-word.

E. INDICTMENT AND DEPRECATION (VV. 11–14)

11. In the day that you stood[32] aloof,

---

11. Cf. Rudolph, *op. cit.*, who has properly suggested that an historical occasion for these words is not given nor needed. They look to a future event. Yet many commentators have sought one. Wellhausen understood these verses to refer to the incursion of Arabic tribes from the east and south in the fifth century. Grimme, *op. cit.*, thinks the end of Edom came by an attack of Northwestern Arabian people called Lihjanites about 475 BC. He considers the word לחם, which has been judged a gloss above, to be a corruption of לחין, the name of this people. The number of older scholars who identified it with the turning of Moab and Ammon against Edom in the reign of Jehoshaphat (II Chron. 20) included Caspari, Ewald, Graf, Pusey, Driver, Giesebrecht, Wildboer, and König. Others who placed it in the reign of Joram between 849 and 842 (II Chron. 21 : 14–17) included Delitzsch, Keil, Volz, Orelli, and Kirkpatrick.

3–4	in the day that foreigners captured[32] his
	fortifications,
	when *strangers* entered[1] his gates,
	and *for Jerusalem* they cast[1] lots,
3–3–3	even *you* were[43] like one of them.

12. But you should never look[22] on the day of your
        brother

3–2	in the day of his calamity,
	nor rejoice[22] over Judaeans
3–2	in the day of their destruction,
	nor stretch[22] your mouth
2–2	on the day of distress.

13. You should never enter[22] the gate of my people

3–2	on the day of their calamity.

You should never look,[22] especially you, on his ill
        fortune

3–2	on the day of his calamity.
	nor stretch out[22] a hand among his goods
3–2	on the day of his destruction,

14. nor stand[22] on the crossing

2–2	to cut off[35] his refugees,
	nor imprison[22] his survivors
2–2	on the day of distress.

This passage abandons the direct form of a Jahweh-word for the much freer form of a prophetic word. Now the prophet addresses Edom, picking up the closing theme of the previous message. The first two lines present the specific indictment in heavy 3–4 and 3–3–3 meter. These are followed by 8 lines in 3–2 and 2–2 meter of deprecation – an effective tongue-lashing which is the most extensive of its kind in prophetic literature.

The indictment is stiffly formal, using infinitives, narrative perfects, and substantive sentences. The deprecation speaks passionately in jussives, expressing sharp disapproval. In both parts Edom's attitude and actions on 'the day' of Judah's distress are the center of attention. This will stand in contrast to 'the Day of Jahweh' in the following passage.

The indictment refers to a day 'when foreigners captured

(Judah's) fortifications, when strangers entered his gates and cast lots for Jerusalem.' The deprecation refers to this terrible day as one of calamity, destruction, distress, and of fleeing refugees. Edom is accused of having stood aloof and taking the enemies' part, of rejoicing, taunting, entering its prostrate gate, despoiling the city, cutting off the refugees on the crossing, and imprisoning the survivors.

Whereas the previous messages have predicted a judgment on Edom, this looks back on events that have already happened, though they seem to have been recent enough still to awaken bitter memories. What was this occasion?[12]

The most probable event is recorded in II Kings 25:3–7. This occurred in 586 BC, about a century before the probable date of this prophecy. The city was besieged, plundered, and systematically destroyed. The king and his army slipped out of the city and attempted to flee toward the *'Arabah,* but they were caught on the plains of Jericho. The plundering of the city lasted a month,[13] which might have given ample opportunity for the actions mentioned in Obadiah. The flight of the king and his soldiers was in the direction of Edom, which might indicate that they had a part in their capture. The historian in II Kings does not record that Edom had any part in the events, however. Two other passages apparently relate Edom to those terrible days. Psalm 137 is clearly a psalm of the Exile. Verse 7 reads,

> Remember, O Lord, against the Edomites
> the day of Jerusalem,
> how they said, 'Rase it, rase it!
> Down to its foundations.'

Lamentations 4:21–22 calls for punishment for Edom in a context of bitterness concerning the destruction of Jerusalem. Neither of the references is clear enough to establish all the details. But they still provide the best available background for these shameful events.

The little nations of Palestine and Syria could fight like cats

---

12. Various answers are discussed above, p. 8.
13. From the ninth day of the fourth month (II Kings 25 : 3) to the seventh day of the fifth month (II Kings 25 : 8).

among themselves. But they still seemed to consider it a family fight. They felt a certain kinship to one another and expected to put up a common front against any outsider or 'stranger.' The main charge against Edom involved her failure to fulfill these obligations of kinship. Not only did she 'stand aloof' while Jerusalem was under siege, an action by which she avoided direct engagement with the conquering armies of Nebuchadnezzar; but in the plundering of the city Edom acted 'like one of them,' the strangers and outsiders. This was the last straw.

To bow to strangers was bitter enough. But to have one's neighbors come to stare and gawk was beyond endurance. To have them exploit that bitter day and even to pocket some of the loot which the conqueror did not want went beyond the boundaries of forgivableness. And worst of all was the implication that the Edomites were responsible for the failure of the king and his fleeing men to make good their flight toward the southern desert.

Through the long years of the Exile the Jews could only lament the deeds in tones like those of Psalm 137 and Lamentations 4. Now the Lord had begun the slow processes of restitution. A remnant had returned – but a very small one. The Temple had been rebuilt – only a very shabby one. But faith recognized that Jahweh was still on his throne. He was still the king over nature and history. And the ritual of the New Year proclaimed this mighty truth. Many things remained to be done before God's promises to Israel were truly fulfilled.

One item of unfinished business concerned Edom. Now the prophetic messages proclaim that God is moving to deal with this matter. It is only one little item in God's great agenda; but its accomplishment indicates that he is still at work, that he has not forgotten, and that he still establishes justice in the world.

F. 'IN THAT DAY' OR THEOLOGICAL EXPLANATION

15. For
the Day of Jahweh is[43] near
3–2 upon all the nations.
As you have done,[5]
it will proceed to be done[9] to you.

2–2–3	*Your dealing* will return[9] on your head.
	16. For
	as you have drunk[5]
	on the mount of my holiness,
2–2–3	will all the nations drink[9] continuously,
	and they shall drink[7] and blabber drunkenly,[7]
2–3	and become[7] as though they do not exist.[19]

These lines fit closely into the context as explanations which relate the specific charges against Edom to the more general context of God's judgment of the nations. This is clearly marked by 'for' at the beginning of each verse.

The syntax, especially the sequence of tenses, is worthy of comment. Verse 15a simply states the fact that dominates the proceedings, using substantives with no expressed verb. Verses 15a and 16a are lines with parallel formation. The first stichos uses a previous perfect to emphasize the completed nature of actions used for comparison. The following stichoi use progressive imperfects to emphasize the action that must respond to their own actions and attitudes. The final line, verse 16b, uses correlative perfects to express the inevitable results, applicable to the nations as well as Edom.

The New Year's festival in Israel was a celebration of considerable importance because it expressed a full theology of Jahweh. Being closely related to the royal line and ideology of David, it built upon his election and the covenant made with him. It took pains to explain itself in terms of this theology. Prophetic oracles related to it did the same thing.

These verses fulfill this function of theological explanation. They are no longer in the speech of an oracle nor the direct prophetic speech of the deprecation against Edom. They are broader and more general in application, repeating things that are already known and reminding the people of the general truths proclaimed and confirmed by the setting of the prophecy within the festival.

The first area of these truths is the repetition of the proclamation that 'the Day of Jahweh is near.' This is a major part of the message that the festival stands for. Whether this is to be understood as the great day of judgment in the festival week, or an eschatological future point in history, cannot be determined absolutely. But it is probably to be understood in both senses. This judgment was acted out in festival drama. But it was also understood that this judgment would be reflected in actual events in history. The speeches of the prophets are often reminders of the sober truth that festal imagery was about to be acted out in awesome history.

In any event, it is the fact that 'the Day of Jahweh is near' that gives cogency, meaning, perspective, and urgency to messages such as this.

'The Day' is to be one of judgment, as shown by the following phrase beginning with 'upon.' It applies to 'all nations.' The judgment on Edom made explicit above is simply one among all the judgments passed out. Or it is an example of the type of judgment that will be passed out. The groups of foreign prophecies in other places serve to make this abundantly clear. No single prophecy should be interpreted as standing by itself, a product of particular circumstances or feelings. Rather, all of them are variations on the theme: 'Jahweh comes to judge the nations,' including Israel. And this theme was an essential element of Israel's faith and worship as practiced in the New Year's festival during the kingdom and afterward.

The universal scope of judgment emphasizes the universal scope of Jahweh's sovereignty which is presupposed in the judgment. He was concerned about justice in and among all nations. The second line of the passage emphasizes this principle of judgment. Judgment will be an exercise of retribution. This is only just and fair. This principle can be applied without reference to special revelation or to special covenant relations. It was regularly used for this stage of judgment proceedings (cf. Amos 1–2).

The third line applies the specific actions of Edom to all the nations as symbolic and typical of their own attitudes and actions. In doing so, he speaks of an action not yet mentioned: drinking. However, the drunken revelry of the conqueror in the midst of plunder is quite consistent with the total picture of participation in the plunder with the conqueror.

The phrase 'on the mount of my holiness' puts the action in a perspective not apparent in verse 15 nor in the deprecation.

Edom's guilt comes not only from committing a sin against a neighbor which would be generally judged as wrong, but also because she specifically desecrated territory holy to Jahweh. In doing so, she despised him and challenged his sovereign integrity.

This act of rebellion, of deliberately flaunting Jahweh and his Kingdom, is one characteristic of the nations. It is the basic point at issue in the judgment scene. What Edom is accused of doing, all the nations do and will go on doing.[14] Edom's sin and her judgment are, therefore, an example of the way the nations act toward God and of the way they will be judged by him.

The principle of retribution is applied within the figure of drunkenness. Edom and the nations have drunk and reveled on the mount of Jahweh's holiness. Theirs will be the fate of the drunkard: first incoherent blabbering[15] and then unconsciousness. Perhaps the latter implies the drunkard's death as well.

In this instance the working out of judgment does not so much imply the formal procedure of accusation, indictment, and punishment as it does the working out of inherent consequences of sin. God is as much responsible for one as for the other. They both belong to the whole process of judgment, to the turning of the wheels of justice. The line gives a generalized form of the judgment pronounced on Edom specifically in verses 4 and 9.

G. 'IN THOSE DAYS'

17. But *in Mount Zion*

14. Manuscript evidence for the text is mixed. Cf. the textual notes. But none of the alternatives actually solves the problem. True parallelism should have a place name to match 'mount of my holiness.' Some Hebrew manuscripts offer סביב, meaning 'all around.' One Septuagint tradition and other Greek texts have οἶνον, meaning 'wine.' This gives a Hebrew word חֶמֶר, orthographically similar to the MT תמיד. But neither of these actually solves the problem of parallelism.
15. The word וְלָעוּ is a problem. It is thought to derive from the root לוע or לעע, meaning 'swallow' or 'talk wildly.' Suggested emendations have included: עלו – 'act severely toward, be capricious or childish'; בעלו – 'to swallow or sip'; and נעו from the root נוע – 'to quiver, wave, totter.' The second meaning of the first root seems most appropriate here, so that it is not necessary to emend the MT.

2-2-2

there will continue to be[9] an escaped remnant,
and it shall be[7] a holy one.
And the House of Jacob shall possess[1]

3-2

their possession.

It appears to have been customary for such prophetic liturgies to end with a picture of conditions which would follow and grow out of the judgment that has been portrayed. The fate of Israel was of primary concern. The Day of Jahweh was obviously not thought of as the end of the world. Judgment was thought of as setting things right again.

Whereas the previous verses were dominated by the emphatic words 'your dealings' (v. 15b), these verses are dominated by the phrase 'but in Mount Zion.' Judgment had been accomplished. At the time this prophecy was formed, the heavy judgment that fell upon Israel in the Exile was still very real to them. This judgment against Edom would continue to display Jahweh's sovereignty in setting right some injustices that had existed from the time of the Exile. But Jahweh's sovereignty was also at stake in the fulfillment of his choice of David and Zion, and even further in his election of Israel and his gift to them in perpetuity of the land of Canaan. Justice would be empty if it did not lead to the accomplishment of God's positive purposes in history.

So the theme shifts to these positive purposes in history with the phrase 'in Mount Zion.' With this the stage is set for the consideration of the state of things with respect to God's purposes with Israel.

The first line deals with the Davidic promise. To David was promised a people to be ruled over by his seed forever (II Sam. 7). It was in relation to this promise that the prophets proclaimed the doctrine of the remnant. Whatever judgment God sent upon his people, no matter how corrupt they became, there would be a remnant, perhaps very tiny and insignificant, which could continue as bearers of the blessing of David and as heirs to the promise.

It may be that the doctrine had its roots in the royal ritual in Jerusalem belonging to the New Year's festival. If so, the doctrines of the remnant and the Servant of Jahweh were very close together. Both were messianic in nature. Both had their *Sitz im*

Leben in this same festival and very near that of such foreign prophecies as this one.

So the review of conditions for Israel begins with the reaffirmation that an escaped remnant will continue in Mount Zion. It goes on to affirm that it will be a holy one. This underlines the messianic nature of this remnant as the bearer of blessing and promise. It will not simply be an accidental particle left over from the debacle. It will be the specially prepared and purified means for the fulfillment of all the purposes of God which had been made so explicit to David, his descendants, and his kingdom. These are the ones prepared to be part of Jahweh's Kingdom as proclaimed in this same festival.

The second line turns its attention to the older and broader covenant. It has to do with the promise made to Abraham (Gen. 12:7; 13:14–17; 15:7; 21; 17:8, etc.) and memorialized in the name Israel. It connects the Mosaic covenant and its promises and requirements with the gift of the land of Canaan, as an influential section of Israelitic theology had done (Deut.). It picked up the theme of reconquest of Canaan as an eschatological theme in the manner of Isaiah 40–48.

The word for 'possession' is מורש. Several translations[16] indicate a similar word, but with the meaning 'dispossessors.'[17] The latter meaning fits the expansion on this theme in verses 19–20 and the difference is simply the addition of a *jodh* in the consonantal text. But the MT makes good sense. Its meaning is theologically more nearly parallel to the first line of the verse. So the MT is kept here.

That the theme of the possession of the land was a very sacred and meaningful one is witnessed even in our time by the zeal with which Israel has been re-established. It certainly is one of the most important elements in Israel's faith and in her hope.[18]

18. And the House of Jacob shall be[7] fire,

16. LXX and Targ.
17. Heb. = מורישיהם – *BDB* – 'their dispossessors.'
18. Cf. H. Wildberger, 'Israel und Sein Land,' *EvTh* (1956), pp. 404ff.; G. von Rad, 'Verheissenes Land und Jahwes Land im Hexateuch,' *ZDPV* (1943), pp. 191ff., reprinted in *Ges. Studien*, pp. 87ff.

	and the House of Joseph a flame,
3–3–3	but the House of Esau chaff.
	They shall burn[7] them and devour[7] them,
	nor will a survivor remain[9]
3–3–2	to the House of Esau.
	For Jahweh has spoken.

The lines before have had a light and common meter. From here to the end they are much more ponderous and heavy. Most lines are tristich, with 3 or 4 accents in each.

This prediction picks up the idea of holiness which will characterize the remnant in Jerusalem. Holiness, like a raging fire, will accomplish the judgment spoken by him who is holy. It apparently is also a conscious reiteration of the punishment already announced in verses 4 and 9. It adds the role Israelites will play in the destruction. In the earlier section Israel simply heard the news or figured as the injured party seeking redress. Here she is the 'rod of his anger.'

The juxtaposition of the names Jacob–Joseph and Esau looks back to the ancient story of fraternal rivalry (Gen. 25–36 *passim*). It is not a natural historical one, for that would more naturally have spoken of Judah and Esau. But from the story of the brothers comes a parallel that cannot be overlooked. Esau's early ascendency is overcome by Jacob's tenacity. It is Jacob, not Esau, who finally possessed both the blessing and the land. Now the wrath that Jacob had feared at the hands of Esau would be reversed as the House of Jacob would turn the heat of devouring anger and in the power of the Lord destroy Esau.

The statement of the fall of Edom in verses 4 and 9 may well be historically more accurate than this one. But the expectation that the final battle for the triumph of God's Kingdom over its adversaries will have the active participation of the saints, does not lack for parallels (Zeph. 2:9, etc.), although other portrayals have them as passive observers of the struggle.[19]

---

19. Isa. 63 and others. This distinction has its roots in concepts of Jahweh's participation in 'holy war' with or for Israel. Cf. G. von Rad, *Der Heilige Krieg im alten Israel*, Zürich (1951).

19. They of the Negeb shall possess[7] the mountain of
                                Esau,
         and they of the Shephelah the field of Ephraim,

4–3–2   and Benjamin, Gilead.

20. The exiles of Israelites in Chalah
         shall possess[4] the Canaanites' land as far as

4–4   Zaraphath.
         The exiles of Jerusalem who are[43] in Sepharad

4–4   shall possess[4] the villages of the Negeb.

These verses make explicit and precise the prediction that 'the House of Jacob shall possess their possession.' It is clear that 'their' refers to Israel and that the 'possession' is defined in terms of the broad promises to Abraham (Gen. 12:7; 13:14–17; 15:7; 21; 17:8), Israel (Exod. 3:8; Deut. 1:8; Josh., etc.), and David (II Sam. 7:10). The destruction of Edom will set in motion a series of population shifts which will return the promised possession to its former Israelite owners.

The verses presume a population in Judah that inhabited Jerusalem, the Negeb to the south, the Shephelah to the west, and Benjamin to the north. It takes account of at least two groups of Israelites from the dispersion who would participate in the reoccupation of the land. This is apparently the region that was occupied in the fifth century BC.[20]

The Negeb is that southernmost part of Canaan, mostly wilderness, which is directly opposite and to the west of Edom. The inhabitants of this rather barren area would be the first to profit by the depopulation of the Edomite highlands. They would move in to occupy the vacuum.

The *Shephelah* is the foothill region of Judah, roughly parallel to the Dead Sea, and set between the Philistine plain and the hill country of Judah.[21] The inhabitants of this area would move into

20. Neh. 11 : 25–36. Thompson, *IB*, V, 858; also N. Glueck, 'The Boundaries of Edom,' *HUCA*, XI (1936), 156.
21. As noted above in the textual analysis the MT lists 'the Philistines' as well. The line is metrically disturbed and the word appears to be superfluous. It can be explained as a gloss which is a textual corruption on the previous word שפלה for פלשתים. But the geographical placement makes

the field of Ephraim,[22] the hill country north of Judah.

The inhabitants of Benjamin are apparently those of the returned exiles living in the narrow strip of land north of Jerusalem. Theirs will be the privilege of occupying the rich pasture lands of Gilead to the northeast across the Jordan. These movements are fairly straightforward and clear. But the lines dealing with the return of exiles present a number of difficulties. MT reads 'the exiles of this army belonging to, or of, Israelites.' The parallel in the next line calls for a place name instead of 'this army.' The antecedent for 'this army' is equally unclear. Duhm suggested that החל־הזה should be emended to read חֲלַח.[23] This is the place where exiles from the Northern Kingdom were sent (II Kings 17:8; 18:11; I Chron. 5:26), and lay northeast of Nineveh.[24] The suggestion has been supported by a number of commentators[25] and has been accepted in the text reconstruction.

With this emendation the meaning of 'of Israelites' is clear. It stands in contrast to 'of Jerusalem' in the next line and indicates that they belong to the former Northern Kingdom, the Kingdom of Israel. The occupation of the land is to take place along broad lines. It will be the reconstitution of 'all Israel' on its land, not simply an expansion of Judaean control.

The MT 'who are Canaanites' makes no sense, so the אשר has been emended to read ירש ארץ. Zaraphath (cf. I Kings 17:9) is a village on the Mediterranean coast between Tyre and Sidon. It is the New Testament Sarepta or Sarafand (Luke 4:26). It is known today primarily for the interesting caves formed in rocks nearby,

sense, and it can easily be understood that it should have been kept in the text. Metrically the passage is better without it, but the sense of the passage is not greatly altered.

22. 'Samaria' of the MT has also been omitted, as noted in the text critique above. The disturbed condition of this text does allow of other reconstruction. For example, Grimme, *op. cit.*, p. 461, suggests that it should read, 'Und das Haus Jakobs wird das Südland (das Gebirge Esaus) und die Niederrung (die Philister) erobern; und es erobert das Gefilde Ephraims (und das Gefilde Samarias) und Benjamin (Gilead).' Parentheses indicate a gloss. This formulation certainly makes the prediction more modest in its claims.

23. B. Duhm, *Anmerkungen zu den zwölf Propheten* (1911).

24. E. G. Kraeling, *Rand McNally Bible Atlas* (New York, 1965), p. 297.

25. Oort, T. H. Robinson, etc.

which have been inhabited even until recent times.

The whole meaning of the line is that exiles from Halah in the upper Tigris valley would reoccupy northern Israel as well as the upper Canaanite plain as far north as Zaraphath. This is a logical settlement since they would be coming from the north anyway.

The problem in the second line turns on the location of Sepharad. The problem was recognized even in the early versions, and a number of locations have been suggested.[26] One early location was in Spain, which was advocated by the Syriac Version, Targum Jonathan, Ibn Ezra, Qimchi, and generally by medieval Judaism. Another suggestion is that it is to be identified with Suparda, which is mentioned in inscriptions of Sargon II and designated a district in southwest Media. Its advocates have included Friedrich Delitzsch, Lenormant, G. A. Smith, and Schrader. A third suggestion is Separda in Asia Minor, advocated by de Sacy, Gesenius, Hitzig, Kuenen, W. R. Smith, Sayce, Barton, Sellin, and the newer atlases.

A new and very attractive suggestion has been advanced by John Gray.[27] He has identified Sepharad as Hesperides near Benghazi of old Berenice in North Africa. The suggestion was apparently first made by Slouschz.[28] Gray suggests that there was a Jewish garrison in that city under the Ptolemies near the end of the fourth century. The definite reference is to the time of Ptolemy Lagos about 312 BC. But Gray thinks there is a definite possibility of such a garrison in Hesperides as early as the Persian period or even in the seventh century.

This identification is particularly attractive for application here because it gives the line such cogency and meaning. As Israelite refugees reoccupy the northern reaches, Jerusalem's exiles will flow back from the south to reoccupy the villages of the Negeb.

The destruction of Edom would, in the natural order of things, only have occasioned the movements in the Negeb. It alone does not explain all the other movements to reoccupy the Promised Land. The fall of Edom is seen as the sign or trigger putting into

26. See summary and literature in G. A. Smith, *op. cit.*, p. 176.
27. J. Gray, 'The Diaspora of Israel and Judah in Obadiah v. 20,' *ZAW*, 65 (1953), 53–59. Cf. also Kornfeld, 'Ob. 20,' *Robert Festschrift* (Paris, 1957), pp. 180–186.
28. Slouschz, *Trends in North Africa* (1927), p. 69.

motion all the actions of God that bring to fulfillment his promises to Israel. His judgment over the nations accomplishes his purpose for Israel in restoring her to her possession.

> 21. Saviors shall rise[7] in Mount Zion
>   to judge[35] the mountain of Esau,
> 4–3–3   and dominion shall belong[7] to Jahweh.

With this majestic verse the prophecy is closed. The juxtaposition of 'saviors'[29] and 'to judge' grows out of the Hebrew meaning of the two words. The two ideas are very close. Hebrew judges were saviors for the people (cf. Judg. 3:9, 15; II Kings 13:5; Isa. 19:20; Neh. 9:27), the orphan, the widow, and the oppressed. Those who are called to save Israel do so by exercising judgment, i.e., by creating justice. Such men judged injustice within Israel and led the people as military men against oppressors from without.

The judgments expressed so vividly in verses 4, 9, 16, and 18 are summarized. Israel shall be saved and her oppressors judged through saviors raised up by Jahweh himself. But their ultimate objective will be neither the destruction of Edom nor the rescue of Israel. Through their activity Jahweh will establish his reign and dominion in history.

The festival themes have gone full circle. From the beginning emphasis upon Jahweh's eternal reign in heaven and the reminder of his majestic dominion over nature from creation onward, the ritual moves steadily to its climax in the proclamation of Jahweh's renewed reign over Israel, and through Israel over the world and its history.

29. Some versions (LXX, Syr, Aq, Sym) suggest נוֹשָׁעִים – 'the saved ones,' as rendered by ἀνασωζόμει, while Robinson, *HAT*, p. 116, suggests המושעים.

V
THE THEOLOGY OF OBADIAH

The theological value of this little book lies in seeing the whole as an exposition of its last line: 'Dominion shall belong to Jahweh.' It exemplifies a prophetic and ritual application of the Old Testament's understanding of the Kingdom of God. Its scope is very narrow, but it presupposes the broad doctrines that were more fully developed in the Psalms and major prophetic books.

Basic presuppositions include those common to the doctrine in the Old Testament. It is understood that Jahweh's universal reign expresses itself in his specific rule over the nations. He determines their destiny. He guides their affairs toward the accomplishment of his ends. In this connection he expresses a concern for justice among peoples as he does for justice between individuals and classes. 'As you have done, so shall it be done to you' is the principle of justice that will play a leading role on the day of judgment, the Day of Jahweh. That this day was relevant to the nations, as well as to Israel, had been an accepted doctrine since at least the days of Amos.

A second presupposition was that Jahweh had a special relation to Israel as his people. This doctrine was typical of Israel's oldest self-conscious interpretation of her role in history. Since Jahweh had chosen Israel, his relation to her was on a different plane from that to the other nations. In fact, this relation determines to a large extent Jahweh's attitude toward the nations.

Still a third presupposition also has its roots in early Israel's faith. It is that Jahweh had promised to unite Israel in Canaan. This promise became on several occasions an element that decisively determined the course of history.

Obadiah uses the occasion of the New Year's covenant festival to proclaim the doctrine of Jahweh's dominion. He concentrates on the one theme of Jahweh's judgment on Edom to do this, but he draws on the full range of doctrine traditionally related to the

Day of Jahweh to do so. Therefore, the little book is relevant to much more than the destiny of Edom.

The first concern of the book is the proclamation that sovereign rule belongs to Jahweh. The Psalms proclaim this rule in the heavens and throughout nature. Other prophecies take pains to sketch its application in all universal concerns. Obadiah applies it to one specific case. But the doctrine is the same.

This rule of God's will must find expression in history. It concerns the affairs of nations and their relation to one another. Since God concerns himself with this subject, no nation can consider itself outside the reach of his power or authority. He will demand responsible action and accountability. Ultimately each nation and each ruler must answer to him.

If the Kingdom of God is to be understood as including in a place of prime importance the stage of history, this inevitably opens the door to many questions. What is God actually doing in history? How does he work? Why does he do (or allow) this and this? The proclamation of the fact of God's rule demands that a key be furnished which will help to unlock its mysteries. For this the reader does not have long to wait.

The key to God's dealing with history is furnished by Jahweh's peculiar relation to Israel. The doctrine draws on the Mosaic and Sinaitic background. Israel's election is not simply an evidence of God's particularistic concern for Israel. It is God's move to accomplish his purposes for all history. The doctrine goes on to associate this with Israel's relation to Canaan, as indeed ancient Jahwistic theology had done consistently. Then it also draws on God's promises to David and the election of Zion. God's relation to Israel, understood in Mosaic and in Davidic terms, has become for the prophet the key to an understanding of God's work in history.

Other nations will be judged by their attitude toward Israel and Israel's king. For in their attitude toward Israel they will clearly demonstrate their basic attitude toward Jahweh. He is known to them through Israel since Israel objectifies Jahweh. Through Israel he both calls and tests the nations.

But the principle also works in reverse. Israel is protected and blessed by Jahweh's acts and judgments toward other nations. Israel's safety and well-being requires that God act to protect her borders and her peoples. Whenever God does not do so, it is to be taken as a sign of judgment upon Israel. But other nations may not presume upon these moments of judgment. For the special relation is not necessarily abrogated, and Jahweh continues to judge other nations by their attitude toward Israel, even in the moments of her humiliation.

Old Testament theology understands God's actions in the world in terms of judgment and salvation. Whenever he acts, there is the possibility of judgment or salvation. Often the same act will mean judgment to some and salvation to others. In this sense Israel's presence in the world provides the opportunity for others to be saved or to be judged. Sometimes Israel is passive in this process, while God judges. But at other times she, or God's anointed in her midst, is active both in judging and in making salvation possible. Obadiah shows Israel in both roles.

These facets of the book of Obadiah are not apparent at first glance. The book demonstrates a view that appears narrow and partial. This is because of the specialized nature of the book as a single foreign prophecy. When this single prophecy is seen within the setting in which it must originally have existed and some of the overtones from this setting are allowed to mellow and fill in the gaps around the text, the grandeur of the Old Testament's grasp of God's rule over all history, which was evidenced most clearly in Israel, his chosen people, and in his Messiah, can be seen to shine forth from almost every line.

LIST OF ABBREVIATIONS

AASOR	*Annual of the American Schools of Oriental Research*, New Haven
Aq	Aquilla
ATD	*Das Alte Testament Deutsch*, eds. Herntrich and Weiser, Göttingen
BA	*The Biblical Archaeologist*, New Haven
BASOR	*Bulletin of the American Schools of Oriental Research*, New Haven, Baltimore
BDB	Brown, Driver, and Briggs, *Hebrew and English Lexicon of the Old Testament*, Oxford (1907)
BZAW	*Beihefte zur Zeitschrift für die alttestamentliche Wissenschaft* (Giessen), Berlin
EB	*The Expositor's Bible*, Conn.
EvTh	*Evangelische Theologie*, München
Ges. Studien	von Rad, *Gesammelte Studien*, München (1958)
HAT	*Handbuch zum Alten Testament*, Tübingen
HUCA	*Hebrew Union College Annual*, Cincinnati
IB	*The Interpreter's Bible*, New York
ICC	*The International Critical Commentary*, Edinburgh
IDB	*The Interpreter's Dictionary of the Bible*, New York
JBL	*Journal of Biblical Literature* (New York, New Haven), Philadelphia
KAT	*Kommentar zum Alten Testament*, Leipzig
K-B	Koehler, Baumgartner, *Lexicon in Veteris Testamenti Libros*, Leiden (1953)
Layman's	*The Layman's Bible Commentary*
LXX	The Septuagint
MT	Massoretic Text
RB	*Revue Biblique*, Paris
SVT	*Supplements to Vetus Testamentum*, Leiden
Sym	Symmachus
Syr	The Syriac Version
Targ	The Targum
Th	Theodotion
Torch	*The Torch Bible Commentaries*
TZ	*Theologische Zeitschrift*, Basel
Vul	The Vulgate
WC	*Westminster Commentaries*, London
ZAW	*Zeitschrift für die alttestamentliche Wissenschaft* (Giessen), Berlin
ZDPV	*Zeitschrift des Deutschen Palästina-Vereins* (Leipzig, Stuttgart), Wiesbaden

LIST OF AUTHORS CITED

SUBJECT INDEX

Kingdom of God, the, 21, 22, 23, 58, 60, 61, 66ff.
Kingly titles, 43

Lake Van, 13
Land, the promise of the, 60n.
Libya, 9
Lihjans, 18, 52n.

Macedonians, 18
Malik-ram, 17
Massoretic Text, the, 29, 35n., 47, 60, 62n., 63
Media, 9, 64
Mediterranean Sea, the, 63
Messiah, the, 68
Mittani, 13
Moab, 8, 12, 16, 17, 52n.
Moses, 60, 67

Nabataeans, the, 18
Names in the ANE, 43
Nebuchadnezzar, 17
Negeb, the, 12, 62, 64
New Year Festival, 11, 22, 25ff., 55, 56ff., 66f.
New Testament, 63
Nineveh, 63
Nomads, 14
North Africa, 64
Nuzi, 13

Obadiah, the book of, compilation, 19; criticism, 7ff.; date, 7, 18f., 24f.; editorial work, 44; liturgical form, 23, 44; outline, 21; *Sitz im Leben*, 21, 22, 23ff., 45; text, 30ff.; unity, 9ff.
Obadiah, the prophet, identity, 23; name, 43f.

Palestine, 14, 54
Persian period, 64
Petra, 13, 48
Philistia, 62
Poetry, Hebrew, 29, 30; parallelism, 29; meter, 29, 33, 37, 46, 50
Prophecy, biblical, 11, 20, 25, 42, 44
Prophecy, foreign, 21, 26, 57
Prophetic audition, 45
Prophetic books, compilation, 19; titles, 42f.

Prophetic oracles, 45
Prophetic tradition, 23
Prophetic vision, 42
Prophets, the Twelve Minor, 7, 20, 24
Psalter, the, 25
Psarhaddon, 17
Ptolemies, the, 64

Red Sea, the, 15
Rehoboam, 15
Remnant, the, 59
Return, from the Exile, the, 19, 27, 43

Samaria, 63
Sarafand, 63
Sarepta, 63
Sargon II, 64
Saul, King, 14
Seir, 12
Sela, 13, 16
Sennacherib, 17
Separda, 64
Sepharad, 9, 64
Septuagint, the, 35, 51n., 58n., 60, 65n.
Servant of Jahweh, the, 10, 43, 59
Shephelah, 62
Sidon, 63
Sinai, 67
Slavery, 16
Solomon, King, 16
Spain, 9, 64
Suparda, 64
Symmachus, 65n.
Syria, 13, 54
Syriac version, 51n., 64, 65n.
Syro-Ephraimite War, 16

Targum, 60, 64
Teman, 13, 48
Temple, the, 27, 55
Text-criticism, 29ff.
Theodotion, 51n.
Tiglath-Pileser III, 17
Tigris, the River, 64
Tyre, 52, 63

Uppsala School, the, 11
Uzziah, King, 16

Vulgate, the, 51n.

74

INDEX OF
BIBLICAL PASSAGES